ANTIGONE

By SOPHOCLES

Translated by E. H. PLUMPTRE

Introduction by J. CHURTON COLLINS

Antigone
By Sophocles
Translated by Edward Hayes Plumptre
Introduction by J. Churton Collins

Print ISBN 13: 978-1-4209-5344-2
eBook ISBN 13: 978-1-4209-5345-9

Cover Image: A detail of "Antigone" from *Antigone* by Sophocles (oil on canvas), Stillman, Marie Spartali (1844-1927) / Simon Carter Gallery, Woodbridge, Suffolk, UK / Bridgeman Images.

Please visit *www.digireads.com*

CONTENTS

Introduction

I

LIFE OF SOPHOCLES

Sophocles, who may with peculiar propriety be called the Shakespeare of the Attic stage, was born most probably in 495 B.C., five years before the battle of Marathon, so that he was some thirty years younger than Aeschylus and some fifteen years older than Euripides. His father's name was Sophilus or Sophillus, for it is spelt in both ways, and he is said to have been, according to one authority, a carpenter or smith, according to another, a sword-maker; by which no doubt we are to understand that he was a master in those trades employing labor, not himself an artisan. It is certain that he must have been wealthy and highly respectable, for his son received the best and most expensive education possible for an Athenian citizen, and served the state in offices which at that time would never have been filled by men of plebeian birth. He was born at Colonus, a deme or village situated about a mile and a quarter to the north-west of Athens, a place now arid and bare and without any charm or distinction, but at that time memorable alike for its natural beauties and for its associations. The Chorus in which the poet celebrated these beauties is justly famous: he wrote it, so tradition says, in old age, not long before his death.

Stranger in this land of goodly steeds, thou hast come to earth's fairest home, even to our white Colonus; where the nightingale, a constant guest, trills her clear note in the covert of green glades, dwelling amid the wine-dark ivy and the god's inviolate bowers, rich in berries and fruit, unvisited by sun, unvexed by wind of any storm: where the reveller Dionysus ever walks the ground, companion of the nymphs that nursed him. And fed of heavenly dew or, the narcissus blooms morn by morn with fair clusters, crown of the Great Goddesses from of yore, and the crocus blooms with golden beam. Nor fail the sleepless founts whence the waters of Cephisus wander, but each day with stainless tide he moveth over the plains of the land's swelling bosom for the giving of quick increase: nor hath the Muses' choir quite abhorred this place, nor Aphrodite of the golden rein.[1]

It was a meet birthplace for a poet pre-eminently distinguished by the fervor of his patriotism and the tenacious conservatism of his religious sentiment. From the hill on which it stood could be seen the

---

[1] *Oedipus at Colonus*, 668–93 (Jebb's version).

temples of Athens, the Acropolis, the Parthenon and the Areiopagus. Within its precincts was the sanctuary of its tutelary deity Poseidon Hippius; to the north of that was the hill of Demeter Euchloüs, and to the north-east the Grove of the Eumenides, where the aged Oedipus rested. Not far from these was the hallowed rift where Theseus and Peirithous slew the victims when they made their famous pact. Altars to Athena Hippia and other deities thronged the central area. Close by, to the south, was the Academy with the altar of Prometheus, the altar of the Muses and the altar of Zeus Morius. Of the poet's early days no particulars have survived, except that he excelled in both the chief branches of Greek education, gymnastic and music—music in the Greek sense of the term including not only what we mean by it, but art and polite literature generally—and that he won prizes in both these subjects. His instructor in music was Lamprus, one of the most eminent teachers in Athens. In 480 B.C., when he was in his sixteenth year, a great distinction was conferred on him. He was chosen to lead the Chorus of boys who danced about the trophy, and sang the paean in the festivities which succeeded the victory of Salamis. This honor he no doubt owed partly to the skill with which he had profited from the teaching of Lamprus, and partly to his extraordinary personal beauty.

His first appearance as a dramatist was in 468 B.C., when he won the prize under singular and memorable circumstances. Aeschylus, the representative of the older school of drama, had long reigned supreme, and had the judges been those who ordinarily decided to whom the prize should be assigned, he would probably not have been superseded by a younger competitor on this occasion. But it happened in this year that at the time of the Greater Dionysian festival—when these competitions were decided—Cimon and his commission had just returned from bringing the bones of Theseus from Scyros for reinterment in Athens. Apsephion the Archon Eponymus, whose duty it was to appoint the judges, had not yet drawn the lots for their selection when Cimon and his nine colleagues entered the theatre to make the customary oblations to Dionysus. It suddenly occurred to Apsephion to impound them and make them the judges. He did so. They gave the first prize to Sophocles, assigning only the second to Aeschylus. Nothing could be more significant than this; indeed it marked an era. The old world was passing away, a new had defined itself. The Athens of Aristides was yielding place to the Athens of Pericles. Of the new world Sophocles became pre-eminently the poet.

For the next twenty-nine years he appears to have reigned practically without a rival, till in 441 B.C. Euripides won in competition with him the first prize, and achieved what proved however to be only a temporary triumph. Of this period of his life no particulars at all have survived, beyond the fact that in the spring of 441 B.C. in all probability, for it is impossible to speak with certainty, he brought out his earliest extant play. But the year succeeding this was a memorable one in his career. In that year the Athenians sent two expeditions against Samos, for the purpose of putting down the oligarchy which had been established there and setting up a democracy in its place. The first expedition effected this, the second was necessitated by the return of the Samian oligarchs, the destruction of the newly established democracy by them, and their open defiance of the Athenian power. In this second expedition Sophocles took part, having had the very high honor of being elected one of the *Strategi*, as they were called. The *Strategi*, who were ten in number, were officers elected annually at Athens, forming a sort of board of which the duties were mainly military, but in part also civil. The word *Slrategos* is usually translated 'general', but we must guard against supposing that it was merely a military office as the word implies in our service. It was a most distinguished public post, to which no mere poet or man of letters without other qualifications and great interest would ever have been elected. The probability is that Sophocles owed it to Pericles, and that what attracted Pericles to the poet was his admiration of the *Antigone.* Such at all events is the tradition, a tradition to which the first Argument to the play lends some color. 'They say that Sophocles was appointed to the strategia which he held at Samos, because he had distinguished himself by the production of the *Antigone.*' We may be sure that what would have appealed to those who conferred such a post upon him would not have been the dramatic and aesthetic beauties of the play only. Without going so far as Donaldson, who thinks that the political sentiments expressed in the *Antigone* were intended as a recommendation of Pericles' policy and that Pericles is in various passages referred to personally, we cannot but feel that in its ethics and politics, as well as in its sentiment, there is much which could not have failed to please that great statesman.

At Samos, Sophocles is said to have made the acquaintance of the historian Herodotus, with whom he afterwards became intimate, and to whom we know he wrote a complimentary Ode. And between the two men there must have been much in common. That the Histories of his friend were well known to him seems clear from many passages in his dramas, most of which have been collected by Dean Plumptre in his memoir of Sophocles.[2] Some scholars think that these passages may be resolved into coincidences, and some contend that Herodotus borrowed from Sophocles; points which can hardly be settled now.

Of the long period intervening between his return to Athens in 439 B.C. and his death in 406 B.C., very little is known. Some suppose that he again served the state in an important office, and that he is to be identified with the Sophocles who was a member of the Committee of

---

[2] See his Trans, of Sophocles, Introduction, vol. i. lvi-lx.

Public Safety, appointed after the destruction of the Athenian forces at Syracuse in 413 B.C. If so, he was in his eighty-third year, and was and had long been incessantly occupied with his dramas and poems, for of the 113 plays assigned to him no less than eighty-one were almost certainly produced during these years. Though a lover of liberty, and disapproving on principle of the establishment of the oligarchical Council of Four Hundred in 411 B.C., he consented to it, because he was of opinion that under the circumstances there was no better course to take. During the rest of his life he had no concern with politics, and is said to have filled the office of priest to a local hero, Halon, the gods granting him—so ran the legend—supernatural revelations.

Before he passed away in extreme old age two incidents occurred which throw light on his singularly beautiful and pleasing character as a man. When the news came to Athens that his brother poet Euripides was dead, and Euripides had for many years been his rival and was anything but popular in Athens, Sophocles was bringing out a tragedy. That the dead poet might be conspicuously honored, Sophocles appeared in person on the stage at the head of his Chorus, both he and they being dressed in mourning and without the wreaths which were usually worn, but which on this occasion were reverently laid upon the *thymele*. The other incident concerns his domestic life. He had two sons, one, Iophon, by Nicostrate a free born Athenian woman, and another, Ariston, by another mother, Theoris of Sicyon. By the law of Athens Iophon was the rightful heir. But the old poet was greatly attached to Ariston's son, who had been named after himself. Iophon, fearing that Sophocles would leave the bulk of his property to this young grandson and availing himself of the poet's great age, cited him before certain officers who had jurisdiction in family matters, alleging that his father's mind had become impaired through old age, and that he was not competent to manage his property. The poet is said to have replied, 'If I am Sophocles I am not beside myself, and if I am beside myself I am not Sophocles.' He then proceeded—so goes the story—to read, in proof of his sanity, the magnificent chorus celebrating Colonus, which he had just composed. Many absurd fictions are told about the manner of his death, to which it is not necessary to refer. It probably took place in the spring of 406 B.C. in the ninetieth or ninety-first year of his age.

By the general consent of antiquity from his contemporaries downwards, Sophocles united in his personal character and temper, as well as in his personal experiences, all that the Greeks summed up in *eudaimonia*, good fortune. 'Dear to the gods as no one else was,' 'loved in every way by all men,' are literal versions of what is said of him by his earliest extant biographer. His long life appears to have been a record of unbroken prosperity. 'Blessed Sophocles'—it was thus that his contemporary Phrynichus wrote of him—'who lived a long life before he died, a fortunate man and accomplished; a maker of many beautiful tragedies, beautiful was his end: no evil had he to endure.' Physically perfect he was from his boyhood upward, distinguished both by the grace and symmetry of his form, and by his skill and strength as a gymnast. As a life, unclouded either by ill-health or reverses, expanded, he proceeded from success to success, from triumph to triumph. Before he had completed his thirtieth year he had superseded in the popular estimate the greatest living dramatist, his master Aeschylus, and had secured a supremacy on the stage destined to be maintained as long as he lived. Scarcely had he reached the prime of life when a higher honor was conferred upon him than had ever been conferred on a poet before; and it would be no exaggeration to say that from this time till his death he was, with the exception of Pericles while Pericles was alive, the most distinguished citizen in Athens. A fuller life it would be impossible for man to live, for he touched life on all sides. In the politics of his time he took, as we have seen, an active, and on more than one occasion an important, part, and was a trusted counselor among statesmen. His friendship with Herodotus indicates another side of his interests. How profoundly metaphysics and ethics with what is cognate to them had engaged his attention is abundantly illustrated by his extant dramas and by the fragments of those which have perished. That he was a minute student of nature and of natural history, is equally evident like Shakespeare and Goethe he appears to have taken his full share of such pleasures as the world has to offer, and, though we may reject with confidence much which scandalous gossip has recorded, there can be no doubt that his private life was not an austere one. The qualities in his character which tradition most dwells on are his kind and easy temper, his modesty and his piety. Thus the epithet which Aristophanes applies to him is 'good-tempered'; while a contemporary poet, Ion, gives us a very pleasing glimpse of him when he was on the expedition to Samos, showing how playful and genial he could be. His modesty is illustrated by an anecdote Plutarch tells. Nicias in a council of war had asked him to give his opinion first as being the eldest of the chief officers present, but Sophocles replied, 'I am indeed the eldest in years but you in counsel': still more strikingly is it illustrated by the charming picture Aristophanes gives of him in the *Frogs*. The epithet, 'most reverent,' bestowed on him by an ancient commentator on the *Electra* is indicative of much which other traditions corroborate. The reverence and admiration felt for him by his countrymen have found expression in more than one epigram which has come down to us. The most beautiful is the following, which may be quoted in the admirable version given by an anonymous translator in Addison's *Spectator*[3]:

---

[3] No. 551.

Winde, gentle evergreen, to form a shade
Around the tomb where Sophocles is laid:
Sweet ivy, winde thy boughs and intertwine
With blushing roses and the clustring vine:
Thus will thy lasting leaves, with beauties hung,
Prove grateful emblems of the lays he sung:
Whose soul exalted like a god of wit
Among the Muses and the Graces writ.

The dramatic activity of Sophocles extended over sixty-two years, and 130 dramas were attributed to him. Of these however, according to the most celebrated of the ancient critics, Aristophanes of Byzantium, seventeen were spurious, so that the authentic canon left him with 113. Of these seven are extant, most of them belonging to the later period of his career. The earliest in point of time is the *Antigone*, brought out most probably in March 441 B.C. Next in order would probably come the *Ajax*, but the date of this play can only be conjectured from internal evidence. Of the *Oedipus Rex* we can only say that it was almost certainly produced between 439 B.C. and 412 B.C., and of the *Electra* that it could not have been produced earlier than 420 B.C.. The *Philoctetes* we know was produced late in the March of 409 B.C. Of the *Oedipus at Colonus* all that can be said with any confidence is that it was produced during the latest years of the poet's life, and was in all probability his last drama.

II

THE PLACE OF SOPHOCLES AMONG POETS

During the administration of Pericles, which began practically in 461 B.C. and extended to 430 B.C., all that was best in the aristocratic and all that was best in the democratic element, met and blended in the happiest union. Never was progress united with prescription so felicitously and harmoniously in the annals of the world. It was a moment in the history of the human race which may be compared to a flower at the very acme of development, in its fullest, freshest bloom before the least faint symptom of decay is perceptible. In politics, the happiest balance between conservatism and progress: in religion, the happiest balance between the old faith and piety which had their root in imagination, sentiment, and emotion, and the more rational and philosophic faith which has its root in reflective reason: in speculative philosophy, the happiest balance between reverence for tradition and experience, and aggressive curiosity: in art, the exquisite conservation, adjustment and harmony of the elements which predominate in its springtime, and the elements which predominate in its maturity—simplicity, majesty, seriousness, truthfulness—blended with a perfection of form not strained to over elaboration and finish, with grace and refinement not degenerating into affectation and over subtlety, with lightness and abandon not passing into laxity and carelessness. But after the fall of Pericles—that is to say between 430 B.C. and the death of Sophocles in 406 B.C.—great and rapid were the changes. In politics a rabble of vulgar demagogues—such scoundrels as Cleon, for example, and the type ridiculed by Aristophanes—turned a rational and moderate into a boisterous and licentious democracy, and Athens became the prey of the multitude. Scepticism and atheism eat into the old religion, and with religion morality also degenerated. One of the most extraordinary features of this extraordinary time is the astounding rapidity with which revolution, revolution religious, moral, intellectual, social, political, moved. It would be no exaggeration to say that between the expulsion of Hippias in 510 B.C. and the death of Socrates in 399 B.C., Athens passed through a succession of revolutions and changes with reference to politics, ethics, theology and art, unparalleled in the history of any other people in the world.

Let us glance for a moment at what the great trio of Athenian dramatists witnessed and reflect in their work. In the world and in the work of Aeschylus, who was born in 525 B.C., we are in the old heroic time when the national religion linked man with the gods through ties of flesh, when the demigods were believed in and sincerely worshipped. In the poetry of Aeschylus it is man and God in direct contact, Fate and human will in awful struggle: an austere transcendentalism is the spirit of his creed: all his creations are superhuman. He found the old creeds alive, and he clung to them; he is radically and essentially conservative. In politics he belonged to the aristocratic party of Aristides who was his hero, and whom he upheld in pleading for the prerogative of the Areiopagus. Twenty-five years of age at the battle of Marathon he is in all respects a pre-Marathonian Greek. Sophocles, as we have seen, was in his sixteenth year at the battle of Salamis. His period of later education and activity falls therefore not in the world preceding the Persian war nor in the world of that war, but in the world of Pericles: it covers that period when the party of Cimon was overthrown by Pericles, and Athens, a limited democracy, was expanding under Pericles. He was in mid career and in full activity when the great city was at its acme of harmonious perfection; he is the poet of the perfect period. His work is distinguished by all that was characteristic of that happy era, and the word which describes it, as far as any one word can do, is harmony. Blending in his imagination the natural and the supernatural, just as in the imagination of his contemporaries it was blended—he stood as it were at the point where faith and reason meet. 'Living,' as Jebb says,

'Just when the old religion had shed upon it the greatest strength of intellectual light which it could bear without fading he is perhaps the highest of its votaries, the man for whom more than any other who could be named the old national religion was a self-sufficing and ennobling faith.' In his ethics and in his politics there is the same admirable balance. In the great speech of Pericles, which Thucydides has recorded, he represents that statesman saying: 'Thus genial in our private intercourse, in public things we are kept from lawlessness mainly by fear, obedient to the magistrates of the time and the laws, especially to those laws which are set for the help of the wronged and to those unwritten laws of which the sanction is a tacit shame.' And this is the spirit of Sophocles' ethical and political teaching, illustrated on the one hand, as Jebb has remarked, by the second Stasimon in the *Antigone*, on the other by the second Stasimon in the *Oedipus Rex*. And so in accordance with this spirit he is not like Aeschylus an oligarchic conservative, nor like Euripides a puzzled democrat, that is a democrat in theory finding democracy in practice a very unsatisfactory institution; but he is not definitely either the one or the other, rather a man who would recognize the idea of free elastic development if only under the restraints of a respected and maintained moral tradition. In coming to Euripides, who was born in 490 B.C. and who was therefore sixteen years younger than Sophocles, we seem to be in another world, because he reflects those sides of the intellectual and spiritual activity of his time, which are not reflected in Sophocles. When he came into prominence the old religion was for many, perhaps for the majority, all but dead. Gods and demigods had passed out of the popular creed. Rationalism variously modified, sometimes as downright atheism, more often as simple scepticism and not infrequently as mere indifference, had now become the vogue. Natural philosophers like Anaxagoras, sophists like Prodicus and Protagoras, and many others who were really disseminating the sort of doctrines and teachings which Socrates was falsely accused of promulgating, were now everywhere busy. Imagination and sentiment were weakening as reason developed.

> The intelligible forms of ancient poets,
> The fair humanities of old religion,
> The power, the beauty and the majesty
> That had their haunts in dale and puny mountain,
> Or forest, by slow stream or pebbly spring,
> Or chasm and wat'ry depths—all these had vanished
> And lived no longer in the light of reason.

And so Euripides became partly a sophistical realist, partly a sad and perplexed thinker, and partly a poet who found in mere art and in the delineation of human passions and afflictions a substitute for the old inspiration and the old aims.

The poet of the perfect period, that is the phrase for Sophocles. His tragedies are, says Müller, 'a beautiful flower of Attic genius, which could only have sprung up on the boundary line between two ages differing widely in their opinions and mode of thinking.' In him Attic drama may be said to have culminated, as our own Romantic drama culminated in Shakespeare. The parallel, it may be added, between Sophocles and Shakespeare, not only as artists but as philosophers and even personally as men, is extraordinarily close. It cannot, however, be drawn here.[4] The characteristics of Sophocles may be succinctly stated thus:

1. As an artist he completed and perfected Attic tragedy by subordinating the lyric portion to the dialogue through the systematic introduction of a third actor;[5] by the regulation of the dialogue through the separation of the *Deuteragonist* from the *Tritagonist*, thus rendering possible the elaborate development of character through opposition and contrast; by making the Chorus the perfection of lyric poetry, and by connecting it with the evolution of the drama not as actively affecting it, but as an ideal spectator, that is as expressing the emotions excited or suggested by the action and as drawing the moral lessons to be derived from it; by developing to its fullest each element in the composition of the drama, the Rheseis (set speeches), the dialectic, the *stasima*, the *kommoi* and *kommatica*, and fusing all into an organic whole, into the perfection of unity and symmetry.

2. So far as the conditions under which he worked and the material which he had to mould admitted of such an innovation, he minimized the Destiny element in his dramas, and endeavored if not to subordinate the supernatural to the ethical at least to emphasize and bring the ethical into prominence. It is this which differentiates him from Aeschylus and which links him so closely with Shakespeare.

3. His dramas present us, not like those of Euripides with a literal but with an ideal presentation of life, and when he said with reference to Euripides, that Euripides 'drew men as they are, but that he drew them as they ought to be', he gave us the key to his presentation of

---

[4] For this parallel see the present writer's essay on 'Sophocles and Shakespeare,' *Studies in Shakespeare*, 127-79.

[5] In the Greek tragedies there were not as in ours separate actors for each person in the drama, but the characters were distributed first, as in the earlier plays of Aeschylus, among two actors called respectively the *Protagonist* and the *Deuteragonist*, and secondly, as in Sophocles and in the Theban trilogy of Aeschylus, among three, the third being called the *Tritagonist*. Thus in the *Antigone* the parts of Antigone, Teiresias, and Eurydice were probably played by the *Protagonist*, the parts of Ismene, the Sentinel, Haemon, and the first and second Messenger by the *Deuteragonist*, and the part of Creon by the *Tritagonist*.

character. 'The persons of the Sophoclean drama,' says Jebb, 'are at once human and ideal. They are made human by the distinct and continuous portrayal of their chief feelings, impulses and motives. Their ideality is preserved chiefly in two ways; first, the poet avoids too minute a moral analysis, and so each character while its main tendencies are exhibited still remains generic, a type rather than a portrait; secondly, and this is of higher moment, the persons of the drama are ever under the directly manifested, immediately felt control of the gods and of fate.' In this we have another illustration of that balance, that reconcilement of extremes which is so characteristic of Sophocles. The characters of Aeschylus, with one or two exceptions, are superhuman, rather colossal types than breathing human beings: the characters of Euripides are merely average men and women with nothing superhuman and nothing typical about them. In Sophocles both are blended but the human element predominates.

4. Like Goethe, Sophocles is a consummate artist, and to the requirements of art everything is subdued by him—passion, imagination, reflection, material, aim. And art, as he conceived it, implied not merely the perfection of expression and form, but embraced all that pertains to the interpretation and discipline of life. This is manifest in the delicate elaboration and infinite suggestiveness of his phraseology and style, which is a wonderful combination of simplicity and subtlety, in the mingled charm and power of his nicely studied rhythm, and in the development of his characters and mechanism of his plots—so seemingly simple if studied superficially, so increasingly complex and problematical the more familiar we become with them. He is the subtlest and most delicate artist in expression of all those who employed the wonderful language in which he wrote. In the structure and evolution of his plays, his art is not less exquisite and finished, and the *Oedipus Rex* and the *Philoctetes* are probably and in different ways the two most perfect dramas in the world. But this is not his highest praise. In the depth and comprehensiveness of his insight into life and into human nature and in the steadiness with which he holds the mirror up to both, in his clear perception of the ubiquity and final supremacy of Heaven-appointed law and of the mischief and peril involved in running counter to it, he recalls our own Shakespeare. But while Shakespeare subordinates theology to ethics, Sophocles subordinates ethics to theology. Never did a poet devote his art to loftier purposes. In his hands, as in Pindar's, poetry became the means not merely of ennobling and purifying, but of consecrating life. Of all poets Sophocles is perhaps the most entitled to the epithet divine. The perfect harmony of his exquisitely balanced powers, the serene and luminous intelligence which is the atmosphere in which his genius moves, his lofty transcendentalism, the steadiness and clearness with which he discerns through obscuring accidents the Real and the True, and

through change and change the Unchanging and Eternal—these are his characteristics. And therefore it was that Matthew Arnold, speaking of those teachers to whom he owed most, thus expressed himself.

> But be his
> My special thanks whose even-balanc'd soul,
> From first youth tested up to extreme old age,
> Business could not make dull, nor passion wild;
> Who saw life steadily and saw it whole,
> The mellow glory of the Attic stage.
> Singer of sweet Colonus and its child.

III

INTRODUCTION TO THE *ANTIGONE*

The Legend.

As the incidents on which the *Antigone* is founded belongs to a story with which no less than five of the extant Greek tragedies deal, and as references to various details in that story abound in this and in other dramas, it may be well to tell it at length.

The founder of the dynasty, to the throne of which Oedipus the father of Antigone succeeded, was Labdacus, king of Thebes. On his death his son Laïus, after certain adventures with which the main story has no concern, came to the throne. In due time he married Jocasta, or Epicaste as Homer calls her, the daughter of Menoeceus and the granddaughter of Pentheus, the successor of Cadmus on the throne of Thebes and celebrated as the opponent of the god Dionysus. His fate is the theme of the *Bacchae* of Euripides. As Laïus and Jocasta were childless, the Oracle at Delphi was consulted, and Laïus was informed that if a son was born to him that son would be his death. Accordingly, on Jocasta afterwards giving birth to a male child, the child, three days after its birth, was given to a slave belonging to the household of Laïus, that it might be destroyed. Its feet were pierced by an iron pin—hence the name Oedipus, 'swellfoot'—and it was taken to the wilds of Mount Cithaeron. There the slave in charge of it met with a herdsman in the service of Polybus, king of Corinth, and touched with pity for the poor babe gave it to the herdsman, who took it to Corinth. It chanced that Polybus and his wife Merope were childless. Hearing of the baby they took it from the herdsman, adopted it, and passed it off as their own child; and Oedipus, having no knowledge of what had happened, but believing himself to be the son of Polybus and Merope and the heir to the throne of Corinth, grew up to man's estate. One day at a feast a youth heated with wine taunted him with not being the true son of his father. The taunt disturbed him, and he questioned his reputed parents, who assured him that what he had heard was idle slander. Still he was not satisfied, and he determined to consult the Oracle at Delphi. The terrible response was that he was destined to murder his father and become the husband of his mother. This he resolved should never be the case, never again would he enter Corinth—so turning his back on Corinth he took the way to Thebes. On his journey at a narrow place near the Branching Roads in Phocis, he met an old man on a chariot with an escort of four attendants, a quarrel ensued, and Oedipus slew the old man and three out of the four attendants. That old man was his father Laïus, and the first prophecy was fulfilled. Continuing his journey he entered Thebes. Not long after his arrival there the goddess Hera sent the Sphinx to plague the city. Perched on a hill near it the monster propounded her famous riddle, and every failure to answer that riddle cost the city a life. What none could solve was solved by Oedipus. The Sphinx destroyed herself, and the city, grateful to its savior, gave him the hand of its queen and made him its king. And so he married his mother, and the second prophecy was fulfilled. Some sixteen years passed by and four children were the fruit of this ghastly and portentous union, two sons, Eteocles and Polyneices, and two daughters, Antigone and Ismene.

At last came the scourge entailed by the crime of which Oedipus had been unwittingly guilty, taking the form of a plague which desolated the city. All came out; detail by detail the frightful story was unraveled. Jocasta hung herself, Oedipus stabbed out his eyes, and blind and degraded and discrowned kept himself secluded in his home till the cry rose that Thebes was harboring pollution. Then he was expelled and he wandered forth into exile, with his child-daughter Antigone as his sole escort and companion. The fall of Oedipus is the subject of Sophocles' masterpiece the *Oedipus Rex* or *Oedipus the King*. Meanwhile Creon, the brother of Jocasta and the brother-in-law of Oedipus, governed Thebes as regent, and Eteocles and Polyneices, conscious of the curse which was on themselves and their whole family, were at first content that he should succeed to the kingdom. But as they grew up ambition was awakened in them, and they fell to feud. Eteocles the younger brother persuaded Creon and the citizens of Thebes to banish Polyneices, who as being the elder brother had most right to the throne. Upon that Polyneices took refuge at Argos, where he married the daughter of the king Adrastus, and persuaded Adrastus to join him in invading Thebes. With them where banded five other heroes who have been so magnificently described by Aeschylus in his noble epic drama *The Seven against Thebes*, namely Tydeus, Amphiaraus, Capaneus, Hippomedon and Parthenopaeus. The great conflict is about to begin; the Argive host has gathered before Thebes, but Polyneices, who was like his brother under a curse from their common father for not having resisted those who had expelled him from Thebes, would have that father's forgiveness and blessing before battle is joined. Oedipus has now made his way to Colonus, his weary wanderings soon to be over—the just gods about to recompense him by a glorious death for the calamities and sufferings for which his destiny rather than his own voluntary acts had been responsible. Antigone and Ismene are with him when the arrival of Polyneices is announced. At first his father refuses to see him. But persuaded by Antigone, in a speech recalling and rivaling in pathos and beauty Portia's appeal to Shylock, he grants the young man an interview, and Polyneices—for he knows that victory will be with that brother on whose side Oedipus shall stand—pours forth his petitions for forgiveness and assistance. The old man listens in silence till Polyneices' passionate appeal is ended; then suddenly turning on him he reiterates the curse which he had years before pronounced on his undutiful and ungrateful sons: victory shall be with neither of them, they shall fall on the field slain by each other's hands. Then Antigone implores Polyneices to abandon his fatal enterprise. This honor forbids; he must go and meet his doom. And so with a parting prayer that they, his sisters, will see that in death he is not dishonored, but has duly his funeral rites, he disengages himself from their embraces and departs to fulfill his father's curse. All this is related in the *Oedipus at Colonus*. Battle is joined—and here the story is told by Aeschylus in the *Seven against Thebes* and by Euripides in the *Phoenician Women*—the two brothers meet in mortal combat and fall transfixed by each other's spears.

Now, as Eteocles had died defending his native city against an alien host, he was justly entitled to his funeral rites, and to an honorable burial. But as Polyneices had died while invading his native state at the head of an alien army, and was thus guilty of the greatest crime a citizen could commit, it was decreed that he should be deprived of those rites, and that his body should be left a prey to birds and dogs on the spot where he fell. Such a fate was regarded by the Greeks with peculiar horror. On the reception of funeral rites depended, it was believed, the welfare of the departed in the next world: in this world the deprivation of them marked the extreme of ignominy and dishonor. Even for the murderer of her father and the seducer of her mother, Electra in the frenzy of her hatred can wish nothing worse (*Electra*, 1487-9). At this point the hostility of Ulysses to Ajax relents, and we need go no further than the debate between him and the Atridae at the end of the *Ajax* to realize of what momentous concern to all relatives and friends of the departed the provision of such rites was.

As soon as Antigone hears of this decree, she determines, in defiance of it, to give her brother the rites which the state withholds and forbids. This is related at the conclusion both of the *Seven Against Thebes* and the *Phoenician Women*. The first of these dramas long preceded the *Antigone*; and the concluding dialogue in it between the Herald, the Chorus and Antigone, in which Antigone, half of the Chorus siding with her, expresses her intention of honoring Polyneices in spite of the warnings of the Herald and of the other half of the Chorus who are against her, probably furnished Sophocles with the hint for his tragedy. At this point the *Antigone* opens. It is early in the morning succeeding the day on which the two brothers had slain each other and on which the Argive army, led by Polyneices, had been routed and driven in panic from Thebes. Creon had succeeded to the throne vacated by Eteocles, and had just issued, apparently on his own responsibility, the decree announcing that Eteocles was to receive honourable burial, but that no one, under pain of death, was to give the corpse of Polyneices funeral rites.

IV

STRUCTURE AND PLOT OF THE PLAY

There are several important points of difference between the Greek tragedies and ours. As Greek tragedy sprang from the Choral hymn to Dionysus and was always associated with the cult of that deity, the choric or lyric part always remained an essential and prominent factor in its composition. The Chorus, the number of which in the time of Sophocles was fixed at fifteen, consisted of persons male or female, who were appropriate accompaniments to the action of the drama. They took no part in the action and in no way affected it. Their function was partly to give lyric expression to the emotions excited or suggested by what occurred in the course of the action, and to draw either by way of commentary or independently the moral or political lessons to be derived from it. In the present play the Chorus consists of Theban elders. In these tragedies there were no acts and scenes, the acts or rather the various stages in the evolution of the plot being indicated by the Choral songs or, as they were technically called, *Stasima*. All that part of the play which preceded the entrance of the Chorus was called the *Prologos*. The first song of the Chorus, sung as they entered from the sides of the Orchestra and took their stand round the altar in the centre, known as the *thymele*, was called the *Parodos*; that portion of the dialogue which intervened between the *Parodos* and the next whole Chorus was called the *first Epeisodion*. This was succeeded by the *first Stasimon*, so named because sung by the Chorus while standing round the *thymele*. *Epeisodia* and *Stasima* thus succeeded each other till the concluding portion of the play began, and that was called the *Exodos* because at its close the Chorus and the actors left the stage. Sometimes the Chorus held musical dialogue with one of the chief actors, and these dialogues had the name of *Kommoi*, an excellent illustration of which we find in this play, lines 808-883, or the Chorus divided itself in alternate musical discourse. As a rule there was no change of scene, the catastrophe not taking place on the stage but being related by a messenger. In the *Antigone* the scene is an open space before the royal palace at Thebes; what occurs elsewhere—the sprinkling of the dust over the corpse of Polyneices and the arrest of Antigone, her death and the deaths of Haemon and Eurydice—being announced and described by messengers. As a rule, the action is comprised within a revolution of the sun: in the *Antigone* it is comprised within a single day. But no condition was more rigidly observed than what is known as the unity of action, which involved the separation of comedy from tragedy, interdicted underplots and the introduction of anything which did not bear directly on the catastrophe and on the illustration of the central purpose, or which in any way interfered with the solemn and imposing impression which the work as a whole was designed to make. How finely is this illustrated in the *Antigone*! In the opening dialogue we see what is in conflict, civil legislation and human piety, the positive law of the state and the unwritten law of the heart; and never in a single scene or in a single incident does the action swerve from the course prescribed, till the type of the one in the person of Creon illustrates the danger of arrogantly exalting the law of man over the law of nature, and the type of the other in the person of Antigone, the heavy price which on earth at least must be paid for defying the law of man that a higher law may be obeyed.

Not less important were the aesthetic and moral functions of tragedy, functions which in the hands of Sophocles particularly it most punctiliously regarded. Its aim was, in Aristotle's expression, 'to effect through fear and pity the purgation of those passions.' In other words, it was to excite legitimately those passions, and by legitimately exciting them to relieve and purify them. For this reason the hero or heroine of a tragedy must not be a perfectly bad or a perfectly good person, because if perfectly bad his or her fall excited neither pity nor fear, if perfectly good, mere disgust: consequently the character must be a mixed one, and the sin or error which led its possessor to ruin must not be a base or ignoble one. How entirely the characters of Antigone and Creon fulfill these conditions is obvious and needs no commentary.

It remains to add that the Greek tragedies were always acted at the two great Dionysian festivals, and particularly at the Greater Dionysia in the Spring of the year, at the public expense. They were produced in competition, and a poet had to compete with no less than four plays, three tragedies, and a farce known as a Satyric Play. These plays might form a sequence, as they do in the case of the Orestean Trilogy of Aeschylus, but they might be on independent subjects, as they commonly were with Sophocles; indeed, he is said to have introduced the custom of competition with independent plays, but this is doubtful.

The *Antigone* was probably brought out at the Great Dionysia in the Spring of 441 B.C.; it is not known what were the other plays in the tetralogy to which it belonged. As the play tells its own story, a brief account of the plot, chiefly for the purpose of introducing the characters and for explaining the point of the Choruses, is all that will be requisite.

Prologos (1-100). The two sisters are introduced, their characters being sharply and elaborately contrasted—Antigone, stern and resolute, possessed and dominated by one idea, the determination to do the duty which affection and piety dictate; Ismene, gentle, timid and feminine. She attempts to dissuade Antigone from an act which will cost her her life, but Antigone rejects such counsel with contempt.

Parodos (101-163). The Chorus describe the siege of Thebes, the unpatriotic wickedness of Polyneices, the death of the two brothers, the discomfiture of the Argive host, the glorious victory over the enemies of Thebes. The chief point in the Chorus is that it emphasizes the guilt of Polyneices.

First Epeisodion (164-331). Creon is introduced, and his harsh, stern, tyrannical temper, which reminds us of Shakespeare's Angelo, declares itself at once in his first speech. He announces his edict—Eteocles shall be honored with burial, Polyneices shall not. A watch has been set to see that no one gives the banned one his funeral rites, and death is the penalty for any such attempt. While he is speaking, one of the sentinels appointed to watch the body—this character is one of the few in the Greek tragedies which border closely on comedy, and certainly he reminds us of Shakespeare's clowns—announces that someone has strewn dust over the corpse, thus paying to it the interdicted funeral rites. In the rage he shows, Creon's intemperate character is further displayed; he dismisses the man with threats of a terrible death for himself and for the other guards if the culprit is not discovered.

First Stasimon (332-382). This beautiful chorus celebrates the wit and works of man, his daring, his inventiveness which, however, can only bring him honor so long as he keeps within the bounds of law—if he breaks those bounds ruin only can result. The application of this to the conduct of Antigone is obvious.

Second Epeisodion (383-581). The sentinel, re-entering, brings in Antigone, who had been arrested in the act of repeating and completing the forbidden rites. Creon asks her whether what was alleged by the sentinel was true—she replies that it was. He then asks whether she knew of the edict. She answers that she not only knew of it, but gloried in disobeying it. Then follows the noble speech in which she justifies her act and draws a distinction between laws issued by mere men and the divine unwritten laws which have the sanction of divinity. Creon, incensed that a woman should set him and his laws at defiance, dooms her to death. But suspecting that Ismene also was an accomplice in this defiance of his power, he orders her to be summoned. She enters, and in a singularly pathetic scene pleads that she may share her sister's fate; but Antigone, who had never forgiven her for refusing in her womanly timidity to take part in what should have been a common duty, harshly repels her. Then turning to Creon and reminding him that Antigone was betrothed to his son, she pleads piteously that the life of one who was to have been his daughter-in-law should be spared. But Creon is adamant: Antigone shall die.

Second Stasimon (582-630). This emphasizes the power of destiny. Woe after woe pursues a doomed family. When from the gods a house is shaken, fails never more the curse. Of the house of Labdacus the two sisters are all that are left; now they too must perish. All powerful is the might of Zeus; impotent the will of man, on whom comes, if the Gods so rule, infatuation and ruin. The application of this Chorus to the fate of Antigone and, in a measure to the fate of Creon also, is obvious.

Third Epeisodion (631-780). Haemon, the son of Creon and the betrothed lover of Antigone, now enters. His character is very finely drawn, and the scene which ensues is a masterpiece. Knowing well his father's temper and the relative position in which they stand to each other, he makes no sentimental plea; but, self-controlled and calm, with the utmost deference and in affectionate solicitude for his father's welfare and reputation, he points out to him that the citizens are not with him in the course which he is pursuing, that it is reasonable to listen to the opinion of others, and that to be unbending and inexorable is both unwise and perilous. 'Shall I, grown grey with age, be taught indeed—and by this boy?' thunders Creon in answer. But still Haemon keeps his temper, while Creon with every word he speaks becomes more unreasonable, imperious, and brutal. At last the young man realizes that all pleas are vain, and, the pent-up passion flaming forth uncontrolled, he rushes out to die with her whom he loved. After Haemon's departure Creon now announces the form of death which he had designed for Antigone. She shall be buried alive; but Ismene's life shall be spared, as, on reflection, he is satisfied of her innocence.

Third Stasimon (781-883). This, one of the most purely beautiful lyrics which have come down to us from the Greeks, appropriately celebrates the power of love.

Fourth Epeisodion (884-943). Antigone, surrounded by guards, is on her way to her living tomb. She mourns her fate, and the Chorus, touched with pity, but lamenting the infatuation which constrained her to fatal disobedience, condole with her. Creon, re-entering, chides the guards for delaying her passage, and Antigone, strong in the 'faith that looks through death', takes her final leave of the world.

Fourth Stasimon (944-987). The fate of Antigone recalls to the Chorus the fate of three others who suffered a similarly cruel imprisonment, and they are commemorated—Danaë, Lycurgus, and Cleopatra.

Fifth Epeisodion (988-1114). On this scene, the most critical in the play, the catastrophe hinges. The aged prophet Teiresias comes with an urgent warning to the king. The Gods are angry with Thebes; they will give their prophet no sign. The city is polluted, and the cause of the pollution is the fact that the corpse of Polyneices is still lying unburied on the plain: let it be buried at once. Creon treats Teiresias as he had treated Haemon before. He angrily refuses to stultify his edict, and taunts Teiresias with being the corrupt mouthpiece of malcontents among the citizens. Then the prophet tells him that for the living soul whom he has sent to the tomb, and for the corpse which he is keeping festering on the plain, he shall atone with the life of his own son. Creon is struck with consternation—never has the word of that prophet been found to be false. His will is broken: he will yield: Polyneices shall have his funeral rites, Antigone shall be saved. This sudden change on the part of Creon has been censured as untrue to nature, as violating probability. Nothing could be more true to nature, for nothing is so unstable and fragile as the firmness which is mere obstinacy, the firmness in which reason has no part. Note, however, that while Creon's unseemly and impious altercation with Teiresias was protracted, the time for undoing what he had done had passed.

Fifth Stasimon (1115-1153). The Chorus, gladdened by Creon's repentance, and anticipating that all will soon be bright and joyous in Thebes, break out into a dance-song in honor of Dionysus. We may here pause to note that Sophocles almost invariably ushers in the catastrophe of his tragedies—it is so in the *Ajax*, in the *Oedipus Rex* and in the *Trachiniae*—by these ironical preludes like bursts of sunlight just before the clouds gather blackest for storm.

Exodos (1154-1353). A messenger now announces the catastrophe, and while he is telling his terrible story Eurydice, the wife of Creon and the mother of Haemon, enters. As soon as Creon had seen that Polyneices had had his funeral rites—so punctiliously were they fulfilled that he even stayed to build a mound—he and his attendants had hurried to the tomb in which Antigone had been immured that she might be released. But on breaking into it a fearful spectacle met their view. Antigone had hung herself, and Haemon in frenzy was clinging to her corpse, a double-hilted sword at his side. As soon as the boy saw his father he drew his sword and, spitting in his face, furiously stabbed at him, but missing him, plunged the blade into his own side, and fell dying with his arms round the dead Antigone. Creon then himself enters in an agony of remorse with the body of his son. But the cup of his misery is not yet full. A second messenger announces that Eurydice has stabbed herself, cursing, as she died, the husband who had been responsible for the death of her two sons. Childless, wifeless, and utterly broken with grief and remorse, Creon prays for death, and cold indeed is the comfort the Chorus can proffer him. He is conducted into the palace, and as he leaves the stage the Coryphaeus points the moral of his conduct and of his fate. What is said it may be well to give in a strictly literal version. 'The first and most important element in happiness is wisdom, and towards the Gods reverence must in no way be disregarded: great words on the part of overweening men get as their penalty great blows, and in old age teach wisdom.'

V

THE PHILOSOPHY AND TEACHING OF THE PLAY

Nothing can illustrate more strikingly the real complexity which underlies and is involved in the apparent simplicity of the art of Sophocles than the ethics of this drama. The central purpose is obviously the relation of the law which has its sanction in political authority and the law which has its sanction in the private conscience, the relation of the obligations imposed on human beings as citizens and members of the state, and the obligations imposed on them in the home and as members of families. And both these laws presenting themselves in their most crucial form are in direct collision. Creon was perfectly justified in issuing the edict which deprived Polyneices of his funeral rites. The young man had fallen in the act of committing the most heinous crime of which a citizen could be guilty, and Creon, as the responsible head of the state, very naturally supposed that exemplary punishment was the culprit's rightful due. The decree issued with its annexed penalty became law, and as the law it was incumbent on every citizen to obey it. In the case of Antigone the other law presents itself at the same crucial point. No private obligation was more sacred and more imperative in the eyes of the Greeks than the duty she undertook, and which, as the last of her race, Ismene excepted, she could delegate to no one else. She had a right to look upon it as a divine commission. She had a right to assert that in defying Creon's edict she was loyal to an unwritten law which had a higher sanction than man's will. Up to this point, then, both are in the right, and neither deserves punishment. Had reason and right feeling ruled Creon, he would have seen that Antigone was perfectly justified in disobeying his edict: had reason ruled Antigone, she would have seen that he was perfectly justified in issuing it. It is not till the interview with Teiresias that Creon transgresses in act and is guilty of sin. He had had no divine intimation before that his edict was displeasing to the Gods and against their will. He is here warned that it is, but he defends it and insults the prophet of the Gods. This is his chief sin, and it is this which leads to his punishment. The terrible calamities, then, which overtake Creon are not the result of his exalting the law of the state over the unwritten and divine law which Antigone vindicates, but are the result of his harsh, imperious and intemperate character. It was his intemperance which made him impervious to the impressions which the conduct and position of Antigone ought to have made on him, which made him deaf to the appeals of Haemon, and which led him to disregard till it was too late the warnings of Teiresias; it was his intemperance which was his ruin. This is emphasized by the Chorus in the lines which conclude the play. But if Creon is punished, Antigone is punished also. Does she deserve her fate? Are we to understand that the poet in his moral does not design to represent that the law which she vindicates should supersede the law which Creon vindicates? A careful study of the play will surely show that he leaves the question practically unanswered, or at all events that what can be urged on either side is so nicely balanced that it is difficult to say on which side the scale inclines. It is important to remember that if a poet is a moralist and a teacher he is primarily an artist. Antigone is a noble and pathetic creation, and the poet has lavished on her all that can impress and move us. Of this effect he has been more studious than of the solution of any moral problem. But on what is now in question let us see what light can be thrown. Antigone, it must be remembered, belonged to a doomed family, and her conduct is regarded throughout by the Chorus as an act of infatuation urged on her by the curse resting on that family: it is defended by no one except her lover Haemon. She makes no attempt to conciliate Creon, but maintains throughout a most defiant attitude, glorying alike in her deed and in its penalty. It is indeed difficult to see how Creon, without stultifying his position and his authority, could have acted otherwise than he did. Antigone not merely braves but courts death. That the Gods did not approve of Creon's treatment of Polyneices may be pleaded in justification of Antigone's act, but this hardly affects the question of her fate. In her case as well as in Creon's, it was not so much what they did, as the temper in which what they did was done, that brought ruin on them.

But from how many different points of view may this most subtly suggestive drama be regarded. It might be plausibly maintained that from the first Creon was wholly in the wrong, and Antigone wholly in the right, which is Jebb's view. It might be maintained that the whole play centers on a beautiful martyr in a beautiful cause, and that Creon is merely the means of bringing about her triumph and apotheosis; or it might be contended that Sophocles had no moral purpose at all, and that the whole play is merely an exquisite work of art. But this is certain, that it exacts and will repay the minutest and most reverent study. Different students of it will no doubt arrive at different conclusions as to its purpose and motive, but the impression most generally made will probably be that Sophocles has with wonderful ingenuity played round a problem of deep and permanent interest, presented it in different lights, and illustrated the mischief and peril involved or possibly involved in any attempts at its practical solution.

J. CHURTON COLLINS

1906.

DRAMATIS PERSONAE

CREON, *King of* Thebes
HAEMON, *son of* Creon
TEIRESIAS, *a seer*
Guard
First Messenger
~~*Second Messenger*~~
EURYDICE, *wife of* Creon
ANTIGONE
ISMENE *daughters of* Oedipus
Chorus of Theban Elders

ARGUMENT.—After the death of Oedipus, Antigone and Ismene returned to Thebes, and lived in the king's house with Eteocles, their brother. But the seven great captains from Argos, whom Polyneikes had called to help him, came against Thebes to destroy it, and were hardly driven back. And the two brothers having died by each other's hands, the people of the city made Creon their king, as being wise and prudent, and next of kin to the dead; and he issued his decree that Eteocles should be buried with due honour, but that no man should dare to bury Polyneikes, who had come purposing to lay waste the city and all the temples of the Gods.

ANTIGONE[6]

[Scene.—Thebes, *in front of the Palace. Early morning. Hills in the distance on the left; on the right the city.*]

[*Enter* ANTIGONE *and* ISMENE]

ANTIGONE. Ismene, mine own sister, dearest one;
    Is there, of all the ills of Oedipus,
    One left that Zeus will fail to bring on us,
    While still we live? for nothing is there sad
    Or full of woe, or base, or fraught with shame,
    But I have seen it in thy woes and mine.
    And now, what new decree is this they tell,
    Our ruler has enjoined on all the state?
    Know'st thou? hast heard? or is it hid from thee,
    The doom of foes that comes upon thy friends?   10
ISMENE. No tidings of our friends, Antigone,
    Painful or pleasant since that hour have come
    When we, two sisters, lost our brothers twain,
    In one day dying by each other's hand.
    And since in this last night the Argive host
    Has left the field, I nothing further know,
    Nor brightening fortune, nor increasing gloom.
ANTIGONE. That knew I well, and therefore sent for thee
    Beyond the gates, that thou mayst hear alone.
ISMENE. What meanest thou? It is but all too clear   20
    Thou broodest darkly o'er some tale of woe.
ANTIGONE. And does not Creon treat our brothers twain
    One with the rites of burial, one with shame?
    Eteocles, so say they, he interred
    Fitly, with wonted rites, as one held meet
    To pass with honour to the gloom below.
    But for the corpse of Polynices, slain
    So piteously, they say, he has proclaimed

---

[6] The starting-point of the *Antigone* was found in the closing scene of the *Seven against Thebes* of Æschylos. There the herald of the Council of Thebes proclaims the decree that Polyneikes is to be left unburied, and Antigone declares her resolve to bury him in spite of it. There, however, she is helped by the Chorus of her Maidens. Her lofty, solitary courage, in defiance of her sister's entreaties and Haemon's love for her, sprang out of Sophocles' imagination.

Though placed here as the sequel to the two Oedipus tragedies, the *Antigone* was, in order of composition, in all probability, the earliest of the three. We find in them, accordingly, some references to it, but none in it to them; no passing hint even at the wonderful death of Oedipus at Colonos.

To all the citizens, that none should give
His body burial, or bewail his fate,   30
But leave it still unsepulchred,[7] unwept,
A prize full rich for birds that scent afar
Their sweet repast. So Creon bids, they say,
Creon the good, commanding thee and me,
Yes, me, I say, and now is coming here,
To make it clear to those who knew it not,
And counts the matter not a trivial thing;
But whoso does the things that he forbids,
For him, there waits within the city's walls
The death of stoning. Thus, then, stands thy case;   40
And quickly thou wilt show, if thou art born
Of noble nature, or degenerate liv'st,
Base child of honoured parents.
ISMENE. How could I,
O daring in thy mood, in this our plight,
Or doing or undoing, aught avail?
ANTIGONE. Wilt thou with me share risk and toil? Look to it.
ISMENE. What risk is this? What purpose fills thy mind?
ANTIGONE. Wilt thou with me go forth to help the dead?
ISMENE. And dost thou mean to give him sepulture,   50
When all have been forbidden?
ANTIGONE. He is still
My brother; yes, and thine, though thou, it seems,
Wouldst fain he were not. I desert him not.
ISMENE. O daring one, when Creon bids thee not!
ANTIGONE. What right has he to keep me from mine own?
ISMENE. Ah me! remember, sister, how our sire
Perished, with hate o'erwhelmed and infamy,
From evils that he brought upon himself,
And with his own hand robbed himself of sight,   60
And how his wife and mother, both in one,
With twist and cordage, cast away her life;
And thirdly, how our brothers in one day
In suicidal conflict wrought the doom,
Each of the other. And we twain are left;
And think, how much more wretchedly than all
We twain shall perish, if, against the law,
We brave our sovereign's edict and his power.
For this we need remember, we were born

---

[7] The horror with which the Greek mind thought of this prevention of burial rites is seen in the prayer of Polyneikes (*Œd. Col.* 1410), and the dispute between Menelaos and Teucros as to the burial of Aias.

Women; as such, not made to strive with men. 70
And next, that they who reign surpass in strength,
And we must bow to this, and worse than this.
I, then, entreating those that dwell below,
To judge me leniently, as forced to yield,
Will hearken to our rulers. Over-zeal
In act or word but little wisdom shows.
ANTIGONE. I would not ask thee. No! if thou should'st wish
To do it, and wouldst gladly join with me.
Do what thou wilt, I go to bury him;
And good it were, this having done, to die. 80
Loved I shall be with him whom I have loved,
Guilty of holiest crime. More time have I
In which to win the favour of the dead,
Than that of those who live; for I shall rest
For ever there. But thou, if thus thou please,
Count as dishonoured what the Gods approve.
ISMENE. I do them no dishonour, but I find
Myself too weak to war against the state.
ANTIGONE. Make what excuse thou wilt, I go to rear
A grave above the brother whom I love. 90
ISMENE. Ah, wretched me! how much I fear for thee.
ANTIGONE. Fear not for me. Thine own fate guide aright.
ISMENE. At any rate, disclose this deed to none:
Keep it close hidden. I will hide it too.
ANTIGONE. Speak out! I bid thee. Silent, thou wilt be
More hateful to me than if thou should'st tell
My deed to all men.
ISMENE. Fiery is thy mood,
Although thy deeds might chill the very blood.
ANTIGONE. I know I please the souls I seek to please. 100
ISMENE. If thou canst do it; but thy passion craves
For things impossible.
ANTIGONE. I'll cease to strive
When strength shall fail me.
ISMENE. Even from the first,
It is not meet to seek what may not be.
ANTIGONE. If thou speak thus, my hatred wilt thou gain,
And rightly wilt be hated of the dead.
Leave me and my ill counsel to endure
This dreadful doom. I shall not suffer aught 110
So evil as a death dishonourable.
ISMENE. Go, then, if so thou wilt. Of this be sure,
Wild as thou art, thy friends must love thee still. [*Exeunt.*]

[*Enter* CHORUS]

STROPH. I

CHORUS. Ray of the glorious sun,[8]
    Brightest of all that ever shone on Thebes,
    Thebes with her seven high gates,
    Thou didst appear that day,
      Eye of the golden dawn,
    O'er Dirke's streams advancing,
    Driving with quickened curb,   120
    In haste of headlong flight,
    The warrior[9] who, in panoply of proof,
    From Argos came, with shield as white as snow;
      Who came to this our land,
    Roused by the strife of tongues
    That Polynices stirred;
    Shrieking his shrill sharp cry,
      The eagle hovered round,
    With snow-white wing bedecked,
      Begirt with myriad arms,   130
      And flowing horsehair crests.

ANTISTROPH. I

    He stood above our towers,
    Circling, with blood-stained spears,
      The portals of our gates;
    He went, before he filled
      His jaws with blood of men,
    Before Hephæstus with his pitchy flame
    Had seized our crown of towers.
      So loud the battle din that Ares loves,
    Was raised around his rear,   140
      A conflict hard and stiff,
    E'en for his dragon foe.[10]
    For breath of haughty speech
    Zeus hateth evermore exceedingly;

---

[8] The action of the drama begins at daybreak, and this hymn is therefore sung to the sun at its rising.

[9] The "warrior" is used collectively for the whole Argive army under Adrastos that had come to invade Thebes and support the cause of Polyneikes.

[10] As the Argive army was compared to the eagle, so Thebes to the eagle's great enemy, the dragon. Here, probably, there was a half-latent reference to the *mythos* of the descent of the Thebans from the dragon's teeth sown by Cadmos.

And seeing them advance,
Exulting in the clang of golden arms,
With brandished fire he hurls them headlong down,
In act, upon the topmost battlement
   Rushing, with eager step,
To shout out, 'Victory!'   150

STROPH. II

Crashing to earth he fell,[11]
Who came, with madman's haste,
Drunken, but not with wine,
And swept o'er us with blasts,
The whirlwind blasts of hate.
Thus on one side they fare,
And mighty Ares, bounding in his strength,
   Dashing now here, now there,
   Elsewhere brought other fate.
For seven chief warriors at the seven gates met,   160
Equals with equals matched,
To Zeus, the Lord of War,
Left tribute, arms of bronze;
All but the hateful ones
Who, from one father and one mother sprung,
Stood wielding, hand to hand,
Their doubly pointed spears;
They had their doom of death,
In common, shared by both.

ANTISTROPH. II

But now, since Victory, of mightiest name,   170
Hath come to Thebes, of many chariots proud,
   Joying and giving joy,
After these wars just past,
   Learn ye forgetfulness,
And all night long, with dance and voice of hymns
Let us go round to all the shrines of Gods,
While Bacchus, making Thebes resound with shouts,
   Begins the strain of joy;
But, lo! the sovereign of this land of ours,

---

[11] The unnamed leader whose fall is thus singled out for special mention was Capaneus, who bore on his shield the figure of a naked man brandishing a torch and crying, "I will burn the city."

Creon, Menœkeus' son,   180
He, whom strange change and chances from the God
Have nobly raised to power,
Comes to us, steering on some new device;
For, lo! he hath convened,
  By herald's loud command,
This council of the elders of our land.

[*Enter* CREON]

CREON. My Friends, for what concerns our commonwealth,
The Gods who vexed it with the billowing storms
    Have righted it again; but I have sent,
By special summons, calling you to come   190
Apart from all the others, This, in part,
As knowing ye did all along uphold
The might of Laius' throne, in part again,
Because when Oedipus our country ruled,
And, when he perished, then towards his sons
Ye still were faithful in your steadfast mind.
And since they fell, as by a double death,
Both on the selfsame day with murderous blow,
Smiting and being smitten, now I hold
Their thrones and all their power of sov'reignty   200
By nearness of my kindred to the dead.
And hard it is to learn what each man is,
In heart and mind and judgment, till one gains
Experience in the exercise of power.
For me, whoe'er is called to guide a state,
And does not catch at counsels wise and good,
But holds his peace through any fear of man,
I deem him basest of all men that are,
Of all that ever have been; and whoe'er
As worthier than his country counts his friend,   210
I utterly despise him. I myself,
Zeus be my witness, who beholdeth all,
Will not keep silence, seeing danger come,
Instead of safety, to my subjects true.
Nor could I take as friend my country's foe;
For this I know, that there our safety lies,
And sailing in her while she holds her course,
We gather friends around us. By these rules
And such as these will I maintain the state.
And now I come, with edicts close allied   220
    To these in spirit, for my subjects all,

Concerning those two sons of Oedipus.
Eteocles, who died in deeds of might
Illustrious, fighting for our fatherland,
To honour him with sepulture, all rites
Duly performed that to the noblest dead
Of right belong. Not so his brother; him
I speak of, Polynices, who, returned
From exile, sought with fire and sword to waste
His father's city and the shrines of Gods,   230
Yea, sought to glut his rage with blood of men,
And lead them captives to the bondslave's doom;
Him I decree that none should dare entomb,
That none should utter wail or loud lament,
But leave his corpse unburied, by the dogs
And vultures mangled, foul to look upon.
Such is my purpose. Ne'er, if I can help,
Shall the vile share the honours of the just;
But whoso shows himself my country's friend,
Living or dead, from me shall honour gain.   240
CHORUS. This is thy pleasure, O Menœkeus' son,
    For him who hated, him who loved our state;
    And thou hast power to make what laws thou wilt,
    Both for the dead and all of us who live.
CREON. Be ye, then, guardians of the things I speak.
CHORUS. Commit this task to one of younger years.
CREON. The watchmen are appointed for the corpse.
CHORUS. What duty, then, enjoin'st thou on another?
CREON. Not to consent with those that disobey.
CHORUS. None are so foolish as to seek for death.   250
CREON. And that shall be his doom; but love of gain
    Hath oft with false hopes lured men to their death.

[*Enter* GUARD]

GUARD. I will not say, O king, that I am come
    Panting with speed and plying nimble feet,
    For I had many halting-points of thought,
    Backwards and forwards turning, round and round;
    For now my mind would give me sage advice:
    "Poor wretch, and wilt thou go and bear the blame?"
    Or—"Dost thou tarry now? Shall Creon know
    These things from others? How wilt thou escape?"   260
    Resolving thus, I came in haste, yet slow,
    And thus a short way finds itself prolonged,
    But, last of all, to come to thee prevailed.

And though I tell of naught, thou shalt hear all;
For this one hope I cling to steadfastly,
That I shall suffer nothing but my fate.
CREON. What is it, then, that causes such dismay?
GUARD. First, for mine own share in it, this I say,
I did not do it, do not know who did,
Nor should I rightly come to ill for it.   270
CREON. Thou take'st good aim and fencest up thy tale
All round and round. 'Twould seem thou hast some news.
GUARD. Yea, news of fear engenders long delay.
CREON. Tell thou thy tale, and then depart in peace.
GUARD. And speak I will. The corpse ... Some one has been
~~But now and buried it, a little dust~~
O'er the skin scattering, with the wonted rites.
CREON. What say'st thou? Who has dared this deed of guilt?
GUARD. I know not. Neither was there stroke of spade,
Nor earth cast up by mattock. All the soil   280
Was dry and hard, no track of chariot wheel;
But he who did it went and left no sign.
But when the first day's watchman showed it us,
The sight caused wonder and sore grief to all,
For he had disappeared. No tomb, indeed,
Was over him, but dust all lightly strown,
As by some hand that shunned defiling guilt;
And no work was there of a beast of prey
Or dog devouring. Evil words arose
Among us, guard to guard imputing blame,   290
Which might have come to blows, for none was there
To check its course, and each to each appeared
The man whose hand had done it. As for proof,
That there was none, and so he 'scaped our ken.
And we were ready in our hands to take
Bars of hot iron, and to walk through fire,
And call the Gods to witness none of us
Had done the deed, nor knew who counselled it,
Nor who had wrought it. Then at last, when naught
Was gained by all our searching, some one says   300
What made us bend our gaze upon the ground
In fear and trembling; for we neither saw
How to oppose it, nor, accepting it,
How we might prosper in it. And his speech
Was this, that all our tale should go to thee,
Not hushed up anywise. This gained the day;
And me, ill-starred, the lot condemns to win
~~This precious prize. So here I come to thee~~

Against my will; and surely do I trow
Thou dost not wish to see me. Still 'tis true   310
That no man loves the messenger of ill.
CHORUS. For me, my prince, my mind some time has thought
    That this perchance has some divine intent.
CREON. Cease thou, before thou fillest me with wrath,
    Lest thou be found a dastard and a fool.
    For what thou say'st is most intolerable,
    That for this corpse the providence of Gods
    Has any care. What! have they buried him,
    As to their patron paying honours high,
    Who came to waste their columned shrines with fire,   320
    To desecrate their offerings and their lands,
    And all their wonted customs? Dost thou see
    The Gods approving men of evil deeds?
    It is not so; but men of rebel mood,
    Lifting their head in secret long ago,
    Have stirred this thing against me. Never yet
    Had they their neck beneath the yoke, content
    To own me as their ruler. They, I know,
    Have bribed these men to let the deed be done.
    No thing in use by man, for power of ill,   330
    Can equal money. This lays cities low,
    This drives men forth from quiet dwelling-place,
    This warps and changes minds of worthiest stamp,
    To turn to deeds of baseness, teaching men
    All shifts of cunning, and to know the guilt
    Of every impious deed. But they who, hired,
    Have wrought this crime, have laboured to their cost,
    Or soon or late to pay the penalty.
    But if Zeus still claims any awe from me,
    Know this, and with an oath I tell it thee,   340
    Unless ye find the very man whose hand
    Has wrought this burial, and before mine eyes
    Present him captive, death shall not suffice,
    Till first, impaled still living, ye shall show
    The story of this outrage, that henceforth,
    Knowing what gain is lawful, ye may grasp
    At that, and learn it is not meet to love
    Gain from all quarters. By base profit won,
    You will see more destroyed than prospering.
GUARD. May I, then speak? Or shall I turn and go?   350
CREON. Dost thou not see how vexing are thy words?
GUARD. Is it thine ears they trouble, or thy soul?
CREON. Why dost thou gauge my trouble where it is?

GUARD. The doer grieves thy heart, but I thine ears.
CREON. Pshaw! what a babbler, born to prate, art thou.
GUARD. And therefore not the man to do this deed.
CREON. Yes, that too; selling e'en thy soul for pay.
GUARD. Ah me!
    How fearful 'tis, in thinking, false to think.
CREON. Prate about thinking; but unless ye show   360
    To me the doers, ye shall say ere long
    That evil gains still work their punishment. [*Exit.*]
GUARD. God send we find him! Should we find him not,
    As well may be, for this must chance decide,
    You will not see me coming here again;
    For now, being safe beyond all hope of mine,
    Beyond all thought, I owe the Gods much thanks. [*Exit.*]

STROPH. I

CHORUS. Many the forms of life,
    Fearful and strange to see,
    But man supreme stands out,   370
    For strangeness and for fear.
    He, with the wintry gales,
    O'er the foam-crested sea,
    'Mid billows surging round,
    Tracketh his way across:
    Earth, of all Gods, from ancient days, the first,
    Mightiest and undecayed,
    He, with his circling plough,
    Wears ever year by year.

ANTISTROPH. I

    The thoughtless tribe of birds,   380
    The beasts that roam the fields,
    The finny brood of ocean's depths,
    He takes them all in nets of knotted mesh,
        Man, wonderful in skill.
    And by his arts he holds in sway
    The wild beasts on the mountain's height;
    And brings the neck-encircling yoke
    On horse with shaggy mane,
    Or bull that walks untamed upon the hills.

STROPH. II

And speech, and thought as swift as wind,   390
And tempered mood for higher life of states,
These he has learnt, and how to flee
The stormy sleet of frost unkind,
The tempest thunderbolts of Zeus.
So all-preparing, unprepared
He meeteth naught the coming days may bring;
Only from Hades, still
He fails to find a refuge at the last,
Though skill of art may teach him to escape
From depths of fell disease incurable.   400

ANTISTROPH. II

So, gifted with a wondrous might,
Above all fancy's dreams, with skill to plan,
Now unto evil, now to good,
He wends his way. Now holding fast the laws,
His country's sacred rights,
That rest upon the oath of Gods on high,
High in the state he stands.
An outlaw and an exile he who loves
The thing that is not good,
In wilful pride of soul: 410
Ne'er may he sit beside my hearth,
Ne'er may my thoughts be like to his,
Who worketh deeds like this.

[*Enter* GUARDS, *bringing in* ANTIGONE.]

As to this portent which the Gods have sent,
I stand in doubt. Can I, who know her, say
That this is not the maid Antigone?
O wretched one of wretched father born,
What means this? Surely 'tis not that they bring
Thee as a rebel 'gainst the king's decree,
And taken in the folly of thine act?   500
GUARD. Yes! She it was by whom the deed was done.
    We found her burying. Where is Creon, pray?
CHORUS. Forth from his palace comes he just in time.

[*Enter* CREON.]

CREON. What chance is this with which my coming fits?
GUARD. Men, O my king, should pledge themselves to naught;
    For cool reflection makes their purpose void.
    I hardly thought to venture here again,
    Cowed by thy threats, which then fell thick on me;
    But since no joy is like the sweet delight
    Which comes beyond, above, against our hopes,   510
    I come, although I swore the contrary,
    Bringing this maiden, whom in act we found
    Decking the grave. No need for lots was now;
    The prize was mine, no other claimed a share.
    And now, O king, take her, and as thou wilt,
    Judge and convict her. I can claim a right
    To wash my hands of all this troublous coil.
CREON. How and where was it that ye seized and brought her?
GUARD. She was in act of burying. Now thou knowest
    All that I have to tell.   520
CREON. And dost thou know
    And rightly weigh the tale thou tellest me?
GUARD. I saw her burying that selfsame corpse
    Thou bad'st us not to bury. Speak I clear?
CREON. How was she seen, detected, prisoner made?
GUARD. The matter passed as follows: When we came,
    With all those dreadful threats of thine upon us,
    Sweeping away the dust which, lightly spread,
    Covered the corpse, and laying stript and bare
    The tainted carcase, on the hill we sat   530
    To windward, shunning the infected air,
    Each stirring up his fellow with strong words,
    If any shirked his duty. This went on
    Some time, until the glowing orb of day
    Stood in mid-heaven, and the scorching heat
    Fell on us. Then a sudden whirlwind rose,
    A scourge from heaven, raising squalls on earth,
    And filled the plain, the leafage stripping bare
    Of all the forest, and the air's vast space
    Was thick and troubled, and we closed our eyes   540
    Until the plague the Gods had sent was past;
    And when it ceased, a weary time being gone,
    The girl was seen, and with a bitter cry,
    Shrill as a bird's, she wails, when it beholds
    Its nest all emptied of its infant brood;
    So she, when she beholds the corpse all stript,
    Groaned loud with many moanings. And she called

Fierce curses down on those who did the deed,
And in her hand she brings some sandlike dust,
And from a well-chased ewer, all of bronze, 550
She pours the three libations o'er the dead.[12]
And we, beholding, started up forthwith,
And run her down, in nothing terrified.
And then we charged her with the former deed,
As well as this. And nothing she denied.
But this to me both bitter is and sweet,
For to escape one's-self from ill is sweet,
But to bring friends to trouble, this is hard
And bitter. Yet my nature bids me count
Above all these things safety for myself. 560
CREON. [*To* ANTIGONE] And thou, then, bending to the
    ground thy head,
Confessest thou, or dost deny the deed?
ANTIGONE. I own I did it. I will not deny.
CREON. [*to* GUARD] Go thou thy way, where'er thy will may choose,
    Freed from a weighty charge. [*Exit* GUARD.]
    [*To* ANTIGONE] And now for thee,
    Say in few words, not lengthening out thy speech,
    Didst thou not know the edicts which forbade
    The things thou ownest?
ANTIGONE. Right well I knew them all. 570
    How could I not? Full clear and plain were they.
CREON. Didst thou, then, dare to disobey these laws?
ANTIGONE. Yes, for it was not Zeus who gave them forth,
    Nor Justice, dwelling with the Gods below,
    Who traced these laws for all the sons of men;
    Nor did I deem thy edicts strong enough,
    Coming from mortal man, to set at naught
    The unwritten laws of God that know not change.
    They are not of to-day nor yesterday,
    But live for ever, nor can man assign 580
    When first they sprang to being. Not through fear
    Of any man's resolve was I prepared
    Before the Gods to bear the penalty
    Of sinning against these. That I should die
    I knew (how should I not?), though thy decree
    Had never spoken. And, before my time
    If I should die, I reckon this a gain;

---

[12] The three libations were sometimes separately of wine, milk, and honey. Here the narrative implies that Antigone had but one urn, but adhered to the sacred number in her act of pouring.

For whoso lives, as I, in many woes,
How can it be but death shall bring him gain?
And so for me to bear this doom of thine   590
Has nothing painful. But, if I had left
My mother's son unburied on his death,
I should have given them pain. But as things are,
Pain I feel none. And should I seem to thee
To have done a foolish deed, 'tis simply this,—
I bear the charge of folly from a fool.
CHORUS. The maiden's stubborn will, of stubborn sire
    The offspring shows itself. She knows not yet
    To yield to evils.
CREON. Know, then, minds too stiff   600
    Most often stumble, and the rigid steel
    Baked in the furnace, made exceeding hard,
    Thou seest most often split and broken lie;
    And I have known the steeds of fiery mood
    With a small curb subdued. It is not meet
    That one who lives in bondage to his neighbours
    Should boast too loudly. Wanton outrage then
    She learnt when first these laws of mine she crossed,
    But, having done it, this is yet again
    A second outrage over it to boast,   610
    And laugh at having done it. Surely, then,
    She is the man, not I, if all unscathed
    Such deeds of might are hers. But be she child
    Of mine own sister, nearest kin of all
    That Zeus o'erlooks within our palace court,
    She and her sister shall not 'scape their doom
    Most foul and shameful; for I charge her, too,
    With having planned this deed of sepulture.
    Go ye and call her. 'Twas but now within
    I saw her raving, losing self-command.   620
    And still the mind of those who in the dark
    Plan deeds of evil is the first to fail,
    And so convicts itself of secret guilt.
    But most I hate when one found out in guilt
    Will seek to glaze and brave it to the end.
ANTIGONE. And dost thou seek aught else beyond my death?
CREON. Naught else for me. That gaining, I gain all.
ANTIGONE. Wilt thou delay? Of all thy words not one
    Pleases me now, nor aye is like to please,
    And so all mine must grate upon thine ears.   630
    And yet how could I higher glory gain
    Than giving my true brother all the rites

Of solemn burial? These who hear would say
It pleases them, did not their fear of thee
Close up their lips. This power has sovereignty,
That it can do and say whate'er it will.
CREON. Of all the race of Cadmus thou alone
Look'st thus upon the deed.
ANTIGONE. They see it too
As I do, but in fear of thee they keep   640
Their tongue between their teeth.
CREON. And dost thou feel
No shame to plan thy schemes apart from these?
ANTIGONE. There is no baseness in the act which shows
Our reverence for our kindred.
CREON. Was he not
Thy brother also, who against him fought?
ANTIGONE. He was my brother, of one mother born,
And of the selfsame father.
CREON. Why, then, pay   650
Thine impious honours to the carcase there?
ANTIGONE. The dead below will not accept thy words.
CREON. Yes, if thou equal honours pay to him,
And that most impious monster.
ANTIGONE. 'Twas no slave
That perished, but my brother.
CREON. Yes, in act
To waste this land, while he in its defence
Stood fighting bravely.
ANTIGONE. Not the less does death   660
Crave equal rites for all.
CREON. But not that good
And evil share alike?
ANTIGONE. And yet who knows
If in that world these things are counted good?
CREON. Our foe, I tell thee, ne'er becomes our friend,
Not even when he dies.
ANTIGONE. My bent is fixed,
I tell thee, not for hatred, but for love.
CREON. Go, then, below. And if thou must have love,   670
Love those thou find'st there. While I live, at least,
A woman shall not rule.

[*Enter* ISMENE.]

CHORUS. And, lo! Ismene at the gate
    Comes shedding tears of sisterly regard,
    And o'er her brow a gathering cloud
    Mars the deep roseate blush,
    Bedewing her fair cheek.
CREON. [*To* ISMENE]. And thou who, creeping as a viper creeps,
    Didst drain my life in secret, and I knew not
    That I was rearing two accursèd ones,   680
    Subverters of my throne: come, tell me, then,
    Dost thou confess thou took'st thy part in it?
    Or wilt thou swear thou didst not know of it?
ISMENE. I did the deed. Since she will have it so,
    I share the guilt; I bear an equal blame.
ANTIGONE. This, Justice will not suffer, since, in truth,
    Thou wouldst have none of it. And I, for one,
    Shared it not with thee.
ISMENE. I am not ashamed
    To count myself companion in thy woes.   690
ANTIGONE. Whose was the deed, Death knows, and those
      below.
    I do not love a friend who loves in words.
ISMENE. Do not, my sister, put me to such shame
    As not to let me share thy death with thee,
    And with thee pay due reverence to the dead.
ANTIGONE. Share not my death, nor make thine own this deed
    Thou hadst no hand in. Let my death suffice.
ISMENE. And what to me is life, bereaved of thee?
ANTIGONE. Ask Creon there. To him thy tender care
    Is given so largely.   700
ISMENE. Why wilt thou torture me,
    In nothing bettered by it?
ANTIGONE. Yes—at thee,
    E'en while I laugh, I laugh with pain of heart.
ISMENE. But now, at least, how may I profit thee?
ANTIGONE. Save thou thyself. I grudge not thy escape.
ISMENE. Ah, woe is me! and must I miss thy fate?
ANTIGONE. Thou mad'st thy choice to live, and I to die.
ISMENE. 'Tis not through want of any words of mine.
ANTIGONE. To these thou seemest, doubtless, to be wise;   710
    I to those others.
ISMENE. Yet our fault is one.
ANTIGONE. Take courage. Thou wilt live. My soul long since
    Has given itself to Death, that to the dead
    I might bring help.

CREON. Of these two maidens here,
   The one, I say, hath lost her mind but now,
   The other ever since her life began.
ISMENE. Yea, O my king. No mind that ever lived
   Stands firm in evil days, but still it goes,   720
   Beside itself, astray.
CREON. So then did thine
   When thou didst choose thy evil deeds to do,
   With those already evil.
ISMENE. How could I.
   Alone, apart from her, endure to live?
CREON. Speak not of her. She stands no longer here.
ISMENE. And wilt thou slay thy son's betrothed bride?
CREON. Full many a field there is which he may plough.
ISMENE. But none like that prepared for him and her.   730
CREON. Wives that are vile, I love not for my son.
ANTIGONE. Ah, dearest Haemon, how thy father shames thee!
CREON. Thou art too vexing, thou, and these thy words,
   On marriage ever harping.
ISMENE. Wilt thou rob
   Thine own dear son of her whom he has loved?
CREON. 'Tis Death who breaks the marriage contract off.
ISMENE. Her doom is fixed, it seems, then. She must die.
CREON. So thou dost think, and I. No more delay,
   Ye slaves. Our women henceforth must be kept   740
   As women—suffered not to roam abroad;
   For even boldest natures shrink in fear
   When they behold the end of life draw nigh.

[*Exeunt Guards with* ANTIGONE *and* ISMENE.

STROPHE. I

CHORUS. Blessed are those whose life has known no woe!
   For unto those whose house
   The Gods have shaken, nothing fails of curse
   Or woe, that creepeth on,
     To generations, far,
   As when a wave, where Thracian blasts blow strong
    On that tempestuous shore,   750
   Up surges from the depths beneath the sea,
    And from the deep abyss
   Rolls the black wind-vexed sand,
   And every jutting peak that drives it back
    Re-echoes with the roar.

ANTISTROPHE. I

I see the ancient doom
That fell upon the seed of Labdacus,
    Who perished long ago,
    Still falling, woes on woes;
That generation cannot rescue this;   760
    Some God still urges on,
    And will not be appeased.
    So now there rose a gleam
    Over the last weak shoots
    That sprang from out the race of Oedipus;
And thus the blood-stained sword
Of those that reign below
Cuts off relentlessly
Madness of speech, and fury of the soul.

STROPHE. II

Thy power, O Zeus, what haughtiness of man   770
    Could ever hold in check?
Which neither sleep, that maketh all things old,
Nor the long months of Gods that wax not faint,
    Can for a moment seize.
But still as Lord supreme,
Through time that grows not old,
Thou dwellest in thy sheen of radiancy
    On far Olympus' height.
Through all the future and the coming years,
As through all time that's past,   780
One law holds ever good,
That nothing comes to life of man on earth,
Unscathed throughout by woe.

ANTISTROPHE. II

To many, hope may come, in wanderings wild,
    A solace and a joy;
To many, shows of fickle-hearted love;
    But still it creepeth on,
    On him who knows it not,
    Until he brings his foot
    Within the scorching flame.   790
    Wisely from one of old

The far-famed saying came
That evil ever seems to be as good
   To those whose thoughts of heart
   God leadeth unto woe,
And without woe, but shortest time he spends.
And here comes Haemon, youngest of thy sons.
Comes he bewailing sore
The fate of her who should have been his wife,
   His bride Antigone,   800
Sore grieving at the failure of his joys?

[*Enter* Haemon.]

CREON. Soon we shall know much more than seers can tell.
   Surely thou dost not come, my son, to rage
   Against thy father, hearing his decree,
   Fixing her doom who should have been thy bride;
   Or are we still, whate'er we do, beloved?
Haemon. My father, I am thine. Do thou direct
   With thy wise counsels, I will follow them.
   No marriage weighs one moment in the scales
   With me, while thou art prospering in thy reign.   810
CREON. This thought, my son, should dwell within thy breast,
   That all things stand below a father's will:
   For this men pray that they may rear and keep
   Obedient offspring by their hearths and homes,
   That they may both requite their father's foes,
   And pay with him like honours to his friend.
   But he who reareth sons that profit not,
   What could one say of him but this, that he
   Breeds his own sorrow, laughter to his foes?
   Lose not thy reason, then, my son, o'ercome   820
   By pleasure, for a woman's sake, but know,
   A cold embrace is that to have at home
   A worthless wife, the partner of thy bed.
   What ulcerous sore is worse than one we love
   Who proves all worthless? No! with loathing scorn,
   As hateful to thee, let her go and wed
   A spouse in Hades. Taken in the act
   I found her, her alone of all the state,
   Rebellious. And I will not make myself
   False to the state. She dies. So let her call   830
   On Zeus, the lord of kindred. If I rear
   Of mine own stock things foul and orderless,
   I shall have work enough with those without.

For he who in the life of home is good
Will still be seen as just in things of state;
While he who breaks or goes beyond the laws,
Or thinks to bid the powers that be obey,
He must not hope to gather praise from me.
No! we must follow whom the state appoints
In things or just and lowly, or, may be,   840
The opposite of these. Of such a man
I should be sure that he would govern well,
And know well to be governed, and would stand,
In war's wild storm, on his appointed post,
A just and good defender. Anarchy
Is our worst evil, brings our commonwealth
To utter ruin, lays whole houses low,
In battle strife hurls men in shameful flight;
But they who walk uprightly, these shall find
Obedience saves most men. Sure help should come   850
To what our rulers order; least of all
Ought we to bow before a woman's sway.
Far better, if it must be so, to fall
By a man's hand, than thus to bear reproach,
By woman conquered.
CHORUS. Unto us, O king,
Unless our years have robbed us of our wit,
Thou seemest to say wisely what thou say'st.
Haemon. The Gods, my father, have bestowed on man
His reason, noblest of all earthly gifts;   860
Nor dare I say nor prove that what thou speak'st
Is aught but right. And yet another's thoughts
May have some reason. I am wont to watch
What each man says or does, or blames in thee
(For dread thy face to one of low estate),
In words thou wouldst not much rejoice to hear.
But I can hear the things in darkness said,
How the whole city wails this maiden's fate,
As one "who of all women worthiest praise,
For noblest deed must die the foulest death.   870
She who, her brother fallen in the fray,
Would neither leave unburied, nor expose
To carrion dogs, or any bird of prey,
May she not claim the meed of golden crown?"
Such is the whisper that in secret runs
All darkling. And for me, my father, naught
Is dearer than thy welfare. What can be
A nobler form of honour for the son

Than a sire's glory, or for sire than son's?
I pray thee, then, wear not one mood alone,   880
That what thou say'st is right, and naught but that;
For he who thinks that he alone is wise,
His mind and speech above what others boast,
Such men when searched are mostly empty found.
But for a man to learn, though he be wise,
Yea, to learn much, and know the time to yield,
Brings no disgrace. When winter floods the streams,
Thou seest the trees that bend before the storm,
Save their last twigs, while those that will not yield
Perish with root and branch. And when one hauls   890
Too tight the mainsail sheet, and will not slack,
He has to end his voyage with deck o'erturned.
Do thou, then, yield. Permit thyself to change.
Young though I be, if any prudent thought
Be with me, I at least will dare assert
The higher worth of one who, come what will,
Is full of knowledge. If that may not be
(For nature is not wont to take that bent),
'Tis good to learn from those who counsel well.
CHORUS. My king! 'tis fit that thou should'st learn from him,   900
    If he speaks words in season; and, in turn,
    That thou [*To* Haemon] should'st learn of him, for both speak well.
CREON. Shall we at our age stoop to learn from him,
    Such as he is, our lesson?
Haemon. 'Twere not wrong.
    And if I be but young, not age but deeds
    Thou should'st regard.
CREON. Fine deeds, I trow, to pay
    Such honour to the lawless.
Haemon. 'Tis not I   910
    Would bid you waste your honour on the base.
CREON. And has she not been seized with that disease?
Haemon. The men of Thebes with one accord say, No.
CREON. And will my subjects tell me how to rule?
Haemon. Dost thou not see that these words fall from thee
    As from some beardless boy?
CREON. And who, then, else
    But me should rule this land?
Haemon. That is no state
    Which hangs on one man's will.   920
CREON. The state, I pray,
    It is not reckoned his who governs it?
Haemon. Brave rule! Alone, and o'er an empty land!

CREON. Here, as it seems, is one who still will fight,
    A woman's friend.
Haemon. If thou a woman be,
    For all my care I lavish upon thee.
CREON. Basest of base, who with thy father still
    Wilt hold debate!
Haemon. For, lo! I see thee still   930
    Guilty of wrong.
CREON. And am I guilty, then,
    Claiming due reverence for my sovereignty?
Haemon. Thou show'st no reverence, trampling on the laws
    The Gods hold sacred.
CREON. O thou sin-stained soul,
    A woman's victim.
Haemon. Yet thou wilt not find
    In me the slave of baseness.
CREON. All thy speech   940
    Still hangs on her.
Haemon. Yes, and on thee, myself,
    And the great Gods below.
CREON. Of this be sure,
    Thou shalt not wed her in the land of life.
Haemon. She, then, must die, and in her death will slay
    Another than herself.
CREON. And dost thou dare
    To come thus threatening?
Haemon. Is it then a threat   950
    To speak to erring judgment?
CREON. To thy cost
    Thou shalt learn wisdom, having none thyself.
Haemon. If thou wert not my father, I would say
    Thou wert not wise.
CREON. Thou woman's slave, I say,
    Prate on no longer.
Haemon. Dost thou wish to speak,
    And, speaking, wilt not listen? Is it so?
CREON. No, by Olympus! Thou shalt not go free   960
    To flout me with reproaches. Lead her out
    Whom my soul hates, that she may die forthwith
    Before mine eyes, and near her bridegroom here.
Haemon. No! Think it not! Near me she shall not die,
    And thou shalt never see my face alive,
    So mad art thou with all that would be friends. [*Exit.*]
CHORUS. The man has gone, O king, in hasty mood.
    A mind distressed in youth is hard to bear.

CREON. Let him do what he will, and bear himself
    Too high for mortal state, he shall not free   970
    Those maidens from their doom!
CHORUS. And dost thou mean
    To slay them both?
CREON. Not her who touched it not.
CHORUS. There thou say'st well: and with what kind of death
    Mean'st thou to kill her?
CREON. Where the desert path
    Is loneliest, there, alive, in rocky cave
    Will I immure her, just so much of food
    Before her set as may appease the Gods,   980
    And save the city from the guilt of blood;
    And there, invoking Hades, whom alone
    Of all the Gods she worships, she, perchance,
    Shall gain escape from death, or else shall know
    That all her worship is but labour lost. [*Exit.*]

STROPHE.

CHORUS. O Love, in every battle victor owned;
    Love, now assailing wealth and lordly state,
    Now on a girl's soft cheek,
    Slumbering the livelong night;
    Now wandering o'er the sea,   990
    And now in shepherd's folds;
    The Undying Ones have no escape from thee,
    Nor men whose lives are measured as a day;
    And who has thee is mad.

ANTISTROPHE.

Thou makest vile the purpose of the just,
    To his own fatal harm;
Thou stirrest up this fierce and deadly strife,
    Of men of nearest kin;
    The glowing eyes of bride beloved and fair
    Reign, crowned with victory,   1000
And dwell on high among the powers that rule,
    Equal with holiest laws;
For Aphrodite, she whom none subdues,
    Sports in her might divine.
I, even I, am borne
Beyond the bounds of right;
I look on this, and cannot stay

The fountain of my tears.
　　For, lo! I see her, see Antigone
　　Wind her sad, lonely way   1010
To that dread chamber where is room for all.
ANTIGONE. Yes! O ye men of this my fatherland,
　　Ye see me on my way,
　　Life's last long journey, gazing on the sun,
　　His last rays watching, now and nevermore;
　　Alone he leads me, who has room for all,
　　Hades, the Lord of Death,
　　To Acheron's dark shore,
　　With neither part nor lot in marriage rites,
　　No marriage hymn resounding in my ears,   1020
But Acheron shall claim me as his bride.
CHORUS. And hast thou not all honour, worthiest praise,
　　Who goest to the home that hides the dead,
　　Not smitten by the sickness that decays,
　　Nor by the sword's sharp edge,
　　But of thine own free will, in fullest life,
　　To Hades tak'st thy way?
ANTIGONE. I heard of old her pitiable end,[13]
　　Where Sipylus rears high its lofty crag,
　　The Phrygian daughter of a stranger land,   1030
　　Whom Tantalus begot;
　　Whom growth of rugged rock,
　　Clinging as ivy clings,
　　Subdued, and made its own:
　　And now, so runs the tale,
　　There, as she melts in shower,
　　The snow abideth aye,
　　And still bedews yon cliffs that lie below
　　Those brows that ever weep.
　　With fate like hers doth Fortune bring me low.   1040
CHORUS. Godlike in nature, godlike, too, in birth,
　　Was she of whom thou tell'st,
　　And we are mortals, born of mortal seed.
　　And, lo! for one who liveth but to die,
　　To gain like doom with those of heavenly race
　　Is great and strange to hear.
ANTIGONE. Ye mock me, then. Alas! Why wait ye not?

---

[13] The thoughts of Antigone go back to the story of one of her own race, whose fate was in some measure like her own. Niobe, daughter of Tantalos, became the wife of Amphion, and then, boasting of her children as more and more goodly than those of Leto, provoked the wrath of Apollo and Artemis, who slew her children. She, going to Sipylos, in Phrygia, was there turned into a rock.

By all our fathers' Gods, I ask of you,
Why wait ye not till I have passed away,
But flout me while I live? 1050
O city that I love, O men that dwell,
That city's wealthiest lords,
O Dirkè, fairest fount,
O grove of Thebes, that boasts her chariot host,
I take you all to witness, look and see,
How, with no friends to weep,
By what stern laws condemned,
I go to that strong dungeon of the tomb,
 For burial new and strange.
   Oh, miserable me! 1060
Whom neither mortal men nor spirits own,
Nor those that live, nor those that fall asleep.
CHORUS. Forward and forward still to farthest verge
 Of daring hast thou gone,
And now, O child, thou fallest heavily
Where Right erects her throne;
Surely thou payest to the uttermost
Thy father's debt of guilt.
ANTIGONE. Ah! thou hast touched the quick of all my grief,
The thrice-told tale of all my father's woe, 1070
The fate which dogs us all,
The race of Labdacus of ancient fame.
Woe for the curses dire
Of that defiled bed,
With foulest incest stained,
Whence I myself have sprung, most miserable.
And now, I go to them,
To sojourn in the grave,
Bound by a curse, unwed;
Ah, brother, thou didst find 1080
Thy marriage fraught with ill,
And in thy death hast smitten down my life.
CHORUS. Acts reverent and devout
May claim devotion's name,
But power, in one who cares to keep his power,
May never be defied;
And thee thy stubborn mood,
Self-chosen, layeth low.
ANTIGONE. Unwept, without a friend,
Unwed, and whelmed in woe, 1090
I journey on the road that open lies.
No more shall it be mine (O misery!)

To look upon the holy eye of day,
And yet, of all my friends,
Not one bewails my fate,
No kindly tear is shed.

[*Enter* CREON.]

CREON. And know ye not, if men can vantage gain
    By songs and wailings at the hour of death,
    That they will never stop? Lead, lead her on,
    And, as I said, without delay immure   1100
    In yon cavernous tomb, and then depart.
    Leave her, or lone and desolate to die,
    Or, living, in the tomb to find her home.
    Our hands are clean in all that touches her;
    But she no more shall sojourn here with us.
ANTIGONE. [*turning towards the cavern*] O tomb, my bridal chamber,
        vaulted home,
    Guarded right well for ever, where I go
    To join mine own, of whom, of all that die,
    As most in number Persephassa owns;
    And I, of all the last and lowest, wend   1110
    My way below, life's little span unfilled.
    And yet I go, and feed myself with hopes
    That I shall meet them, by my father loved,
    Dear to my mother, well-beloved of thee,
    Thou dearest brother: I, with these my hands,
    Washed each dear corpse, arrayed you, poured the stream,
    In rites of burial. And in care for thee,
    Thy body, Polynices, honouring,
    I gain this recompense. And yet 'twas well;
    I had not done it had I come to be   1120
    A mother with her children,—had not dared,
    Though 'twere a husband dead that mouldered there,
    Against my country's will to bear this toil,
    And dost thou ask what law constrained me thus?
    I answer, had I lost a husband dear,
    I might have had another; other sons
    By other spouse, if one were lost to me;
    But when my father and my mother sleep
    In Hades, then no brother more can come.
    And therefore, giving thee the foremost place,   1130
    I seemed in Creon's eyes, O brother dear,
    To sin in boldest daring. So himself,
    He leads me, having taken me by force,

Cut off from marriage bed and marriage feast,
Untasting wife's true joy, or mother's bliss,
With infant at her breast, but all forlorn,
Bereaved of friends, in utter misery,
Alive, I tread the chambers of the dead.
What law of Heaven have I transgressed against?
What use for me, ill-starred one, still to look   1140
To any God for succour, or to call
On any friend for aid? For holiest deed
I bear this charge of rank unholiness.
If acts like these the Gods on high approve,
We, taught by suffering, own that we have sinned;
But if they sin [*looking at* CREON], I pray they suffer not
Worse evils than the wrongs they do to me.
CHORUS. Still do the same wild blasts
    Vex her poor storm-tossed soul.
CREON. Therefore shall these her guards   1150
    Weep sore for this delay.
ANTIGONE. Ah me! this word of thine
    Tells of death drawing nigh.
CREON. I cannot bid thee hope
    That other fate is thine.
ANTIGONE. O citadel of Thebes, my native land,
    Ye Gods of old renown,
    I go, and linger not.
    Behold me. O ye senators of Thebes,
    The last, love scion of the kingly race,   1160
    What things I suffer, and from whom they come,
    Revering still where reverence most is due.

[*Guards lead* ANTIGONE *away.*]

STROPHE. I

CHORUS. So Danæ's form endured of old,[14]
    In brazen palace hid,
    To lose the light of heaven,
    And in her tomblike chamber was enclosed,
    And yet high honour came to her, O child,
    And on her flowed the golden shower of Zeus.
    But great and dread the might of Destiny:

---

[14] As Antigone had gone back to the parallelisms of the past, so does the Chorus, finding in the first, at least, of the three examples that follow some topic of consolation. Danae, though shut up by her father Acrisios, received the golden shower of Zeus, and became the mother of the hero Perseus.

Nor tempest-storm, nor war,   1170
Nor tower, nor dark-hulled ships
That sweep the sea, escape.

ANTISTROPHE. I

Bitter and sharp in mood,
The son of Dryas,[15] king
Of yon Edonian tribes,
By Dionysus' hands,
Was shut in prison cave,
And so his frenzy wild and soul o'erbold
Waste slowly evermore.
And he was taught that he, with ribald tongue   1180
In what wild frenzy, had attacked the Gods.
For fain had he the Mænad throng brought low,
And that bright flashing fire,
And roused the wrath of Muses sweet in song.

STROPHE. II

And by Kyanean waters' double sea[16]
Are shores of Bosphorus, and Thracian isle,
As Salmydessus known, inhospitable,
Where Ares, God of all the region round,
Saw the accursed wound
That smote with blindness Phineus' twin-born sons   1190
By a fierce stepdame's hand,—
Dark wound, upon the dark-doomed eyeballs struck,
Not with the stroke of sword,
But blood-stained hands, on point of spindle sharp.

---

[15] The son of Dryas was Lycurgos, who appears in the Iliad, vi. 130, as having, like Pentheus, opposed the worship of Dionysos, and so fallen under the wrath of Zeus, who deprived him of sight, and entombed him in a cavern. The Muses are here mentioned as the companions and nurses of Dionysos.

[16] The last instance was taken from the early legends of Attica. Boreas, it was said, carried off Oreithyia, daughter of Erechtheus, and by her had two sons and a daughter, Cleopatra. The latter became the wife of Phineus, king of Salmydessos, and bore two sons to him, Plexippos and Pandion. Phineus then divorced her, married another wife, Idæa, and then, at her instigation, deprived his two sons by the former marriage of their sight, and confined Cleopatra in a dungeon. She too, like Danae and Niobe, was "a child of Gods," and the Erechtheion on the Acropolis was consecrated to the joint worship of her grandfather and of Poseidon.

ANTISTROPHE. II

And they in misery, miserable fate
Lamenting, waste away,
Born of a mother wedded to a curse.
And she who claimed descent
From men of ancient fame,
The old Erechteid race,   1200
Daughter of Boreas, in far distant caves
Amid her father's woods,
Was reared, a child of Gods,
Swift moving as the steed, o'er lofty crag,
And yet, my child, on her
   Bore down the Destinies,
   Whose years are infinite.

[*Enter* TEIRESIAS, *guided by a* Boy.]

TEIRESIAS. Princes of Thebes, we come as travellers joined,
   One seeing for both, for still the blind must use
   A guide's assistance to direct his steps.   1210
CREON. And what new thing, Teiresias, brings thee here?
TEIRESIAS. That I will tell thee, and do thou obey
   The seer who speaks.
CREON. Of old I was not wont
   To differ from thy judgment.
TEIRESIAS. Therefore, well
   And safely dost thou steer our good ship's course.
CREON. I, from experience, bear my witness still
   Of good derived from thee.
TEIRESIAS. Bethink thee, then,   1220
   Thou walkest now upon a razor's edge.
CREON. What means this? Lo! I shudder at thy speech.
TEIRESIAS. Soon shalt thou know, as I unfold the signs
   Of my dread art. For sitting, as of old,
   Upon my ancient seat of augury,
   Where every bird has access, lo! I hear
   Strange cry of winged creatures, shouting shrill,
   In clamour sharp and savage, and I knew
   That they were tearing each the other's breast
   With bloody talons, for their whirring wings   1230
   Made that quite clear; and straightway I, in fear,
   Made trial of the sacrifice that lay
   On fiery altar. But the living flame

Shone not from out the offering; then there oozed
Upon the ashes, trickling from the bones,
A moisture, and it bubbled, and it spat,
And, lo! the gall was scattered to the air,
And forth from out the fat that wrapped them round,
The thigh joints fell. Such omens of decay
From strange mysterious rites I learnt from him,   1240
This boy, who now stands here, for he is still
A guide to me, as I to others am.
And all this evil falls upon the state,
From out thy counsels; for our altars all,
Our sacred hearths, are full of food for dogs
And birds unclean, the flesh of that poor wretch
Who fell, the son of Oedipus. And so
The Gods no longer hear our solemn prayers,
Nor own the flame that burns the sacrifice;
Nor do the birds give cry of omen good,   1250
But feed on carrion of a human corpse.
Think thou on this, my son: to err, indeed,
Is common unto all, but having erred,
He is no longer reckless or unblest,
Who, having fallen into evil, seeks
For healing, nor continues still unmoved.
Self-will must bear the guilt of stubbornness:
Yield to the dead, and outrage not a corpse.
What gain is it a fallen foe to slay?
Good counsel give I, planning good for thee;   1260
And of all joys the sweetest is to learn
From one who speaketh well, should that bring gain.
CREON. Old man, as archers aiming at their mark,
So ye shoot forth your venomed darts at me;
I know your augur's skill, and by your arts
Long since am tricked and sold. Yes, gain your gains,
Get precious bronze from Sardis, Indian gold,[17]
That corpse ye shall not hide in any tomb.
Not though the eagles, birds of Zeus, should bear
Their carrion morsels to their master's throne,   1270
Not even fearing this pollution dire,
Will I consent to burial. Well I know
That man is powerless to pollute the Gods.
But many fall, Teiresias, dotard old,

---

[17] The precise nature of the *electron* of the Greek is doubtful; but Sardis leads us to think of the gold dust of Pactolos, and the name of some characteristic distinguishing it from other gold.

A shameful fall, who gloze their shameful words,
For lucre's sake, with surface show of good.
TEIRESIAS. Ah, me! Does no man know, does none consider....
CREON. Consider what? What trite poor saw is this?
TEIRESIAS. How far good counsel heaped up wealth excels?
CREON. By just so far methinks the greatest hurt   1280
Is sheer unwisdom.
TEIRESIAS. Thou, at least, hast grown
From head to foot all full of that disease.
CREON. Loath am I with a prophet evil words
To bandy to and fro.
TEIRESIAS. And yet thou dost so,
Saying that I utter speech that is not true.
CREON. The race of seers is ever fond of gold.
TEIRESIAS. And that of tyrants loves the gain that comes
Of filthy lucre.   1290
CREON. Art thou ignorant, then,
That what thou say'st, thou speak'st of those that rule?
TEIRESIAS. I know it. 'Twas from me thou hadst the state,
By me preserved.
CREON. Wise art thou as a seer,
But too much given to wrong and injury.
TEIRESIAS. Thou wilt provoke me in my wrath to speak
Of things best left unspoken.
CREON. Speak them out!
Only take heed thou speak them not for gain.   1300
TEIRESIAS. And dost thou, then, already judge me thus?
CREON. Know that my judgment is not bought and sold.
TEIRESIAS. Know, then, and know it well, that thou shalt see
Not many winding circuits of the sun,
Before thou giv'st a quittance for the dead,
A corpse by thee begotten; for that thou
Hast trampled to the ground what stood on high,
And foully placed within a charnel-house
A living soul. And now thou keep'st from them,
The Gods below, the corpse of one unblest,   1310
Unwept, unhallowed. Neither part nor lot
Hast thou in them, nor have the Gods who rule
The worlds above, but at thy hands they meet
This outrage. And for this they wait for thee,
The sure though slow avengers of the grave,
The dread Erinyes of the Gods above,
In these same evils to be snared and caught.
Search well if I say this as one who sells
His soul for money. Yet a little while,

And in thy house men's wailing, women's cry,   1320
Shall make it plain. And every city stirs
Itself in arms against thee, owning those
Whose limbs the dogs have buried, or fierce wolves,
Or wingèd birds have brought the accursèd taint
To city's altar-hearth. Doom like to this,
Sure darting as an arrow to its mark,
I launch at thee (for thou dost grieve me sore),
An archer aiming at the very heart,
And thou shalt not escape its fiery sting.
And now, O boy, lead thou me home again,   1330
And let him vent his spleen on younger men,
And learn to keep his tongue more orderly,
With better thoughts than this his present mood. [*Exit.*]
CHORUS. The man has gone, O king, predicting woe,
    And well we know, since first our raven hair
    Was mixed with gray, that never yet his words
    Were uttered to our state and failed of truth.
CREON. I know it too, 'tis that that troubles me.
    To yield is hard, but, holding out, to smite
    One's soul with sorrow, this is harder still.   1340
CHORUS. Much need is there, O Creon, at this hour,
    Of wisest counsel.
CREON. What, then, should I do?
    Tell me and I will hearken.
CHORUS. Go thou first,
    Release the maiden from her cavern tomb,
    And give a grave to him who lies exposed.
CREON. Is this thy counsel? Dost thou bid me yield?
CHORUS. Without delay, O king, for, lo! they come,
    The God's swift-footed ministers of ill,   1350
    And in an instant lay the wicked low.
CREON. Ah, me! 'tis hard; and yet I bend my will
    To do thy bidding. With necessity
    We must not fight at such o'erwhelming odds.
CHORUS. Go, then, and act! Commit it not to others.
CREON. E'en as I am I'll go. Come, come, my men,
    Present or absent, come, and in your hands
    Bring axes. Come to yonder eminence,
    And I, since now my judgment leans that way,
    Who myself bound her, now myself will loose.   1360
    Too much I fear lest it should wisest prove
    To end my life, maintaining ancient laws. [*Exit.*]

STROPHE. I

CHORUS. O thou of many names,[18]
    Of that Cadmeian maid[19]
    The glory and the joy,
    Child of loud-thundering Zeus,
    Who watchest over fair Italia,[20]
    And reign'st o'er all the bays that open wide,
    Which Deo claims on fair Eleusis' coast:[21]
    Bacchus, who dwell'st in Thebes,   1370
    The mother city of thy Bacchant train,
    Among Ismenus' stream that glideth on,
    And with the dragon's brood;[22]

ANTISTROPHE. I

    Thee, o'er the double peak of yonder height,
    The flashing blaze beholds,
    Where nymphs of Corycus[23]
    Go forth in Bacchic dance,
    And by Castalia's stream;
    And thee the ivied slopes of Nysa's hills,[24]
    And vine-clad promontory,   1380
    While words of more than mortal melody
    Shout out the well-known name,
    Send forth, the guardian lord
    Of all the streets of Thebes.

---

[18] The exulting hopes of the Chorus, rising out of Creon's repentance, seem purposely brought into contrast with the tragedy which is passing while they are in the very act of chanting their hymns.

[19] The Cadmeian maid is Semele, the bride of Zeus, who perished when the God revealed himself as the thunderer.

[20] Southern Italy, the Magna Græcia of the old geographers, is named as famous both for its wines and its *cultus* of Bacchos, perhaps also with a special allusion to the foundation of Thurii by the Athenians.

[21] Here, as in *Œd. Col.* (680), the poet speaks as one who had been initiated in the mysteries of Eleusis, where Bacchos, under the name Iacchos, received a special adoration.

[22] The people descended from the dragon's teeth sown by Cadmos.

[23] From Italia and Eleusis the Chorus passes to Parnassos, as the centre of the Bacchic *cultus*. On the twin peaks of that mountain flames were said to have been seen, telling of the presence of the God.

[24] The "ivied slopes" are those of the Eubœan Nysa, where grew the wondrous vine described in Fragm. 235.

STROPHE. II

Above all cities thou,
With her, thy mother, whom the thunder slew,
Dost look on it with love;
And now, since all the city bendeth low
Beneath the sullen plague,
Come thou with cleansing tread   1390
O'er the Parnassian slopes,
Or o'er the moaning straits.[25]

ANTISTROPHE. II

O thou, who lead'st the band
Of stars still breathing fire,[26]
Lord of the hymns that echo in the night,
Offspring of highest Zeus,
Appear, we pray thee, with thy Naxian train,
Of Thyian maidens, frenzied, passionate,
Who all night long, in maddening chorus, sing
Thy praise, their lord, Iacchus.   1400

[*Enter* MESSENGER.]

MESSENGER. Ye men of Cadmus and Amphion's house,[27]
    I know no life of mortal man which I
    Would either praise or blame. It is but chance
    That raiseth up, and chance that bringeth low,
    The man who lives in good or evil plight,
    And none foretells a man's appointed lot.
    For Creon, in my judgment, men might watch
    With envy and with wonder, having saved
    This land of Cadmus from the bands of foes;
    And, having ruled with fullest sovereignty,   1410
    He lived and prospered, joyous in a race
    Of goodly offspring. Now, all this is gone;

---

[25] The "moaning straits" of the Euripos, if the God is thought of as coming from Nysa, the "slopes," if he comes from Parnassos.

[26] The imagery of the Bacchic *thiasos,* with its torch-bearers moving in rhythmic order, is transferred to the heavens, and the stars themselves are thought of as a choral band led by the Lord of life and joy.

[27] In the myths of the foundation of Thebes, Amphion was said to have built its walls by the mere power of his minstrelsy, the stones moving, as he played, each into its appointed place.

For when men lose the joys that sweeten life,
I cannot count this living, rather deem
As of a breathing corpse. His heaped-up stores
Of wealth are large; so be it, and he lives
With all a sovereign's state, and yet, if joy
Be absent, all the rest I count as naught,
And would not weigh them against pleasure's charm,
More than a vapour's shadow.   1420

CHORUS. What is this?
What new disaster tell'st thou of our chiefs?

MESSENGER. Dead are they, and the living cause their death.

CHORUS. Who slays, and who is slaughtered? Tell thy tale.

MESSENGER. Haemon is dead. His own hand sheds his blood.

CHORUS. Was it father's hand that struck the blow,
Or his own arm?

MESSENGER. He by himself alone,
Yet in his wrath he charged his father with it.

CHORUS. O prophet! true, most true, those words of thine.   1430

MESSENGER. Since thus it stands, we may as well debate
Of other things in council.

CHORUS. Lo! there comes
The wife of Creon, sad Eurydice.
She from the house is come, or hearing speech
About her son, or else by chance.

[*Enter* EURYDICE.]

EURYDICE. My friends,
I on my way without, as suppliant bound
To pay my vows at Pallas' shrine, have heard
Your words, and so I chanced to slip the bolt   1440
Of the half-opened door, when, lo! a sound
Falls on my ears of evil near at hand,
And terror-struck I fell in deadly swoon
Back in my handmaids' arms; yet tell it me,
Tell the tale once again, for I shall hear,
By long experience disciplined to grief.

MESSENGER. Dear lady, I will tell thee: I was by,
And will not leave one word of truth untold.
Why should we smooth and gloze, when all too soon
We should be found as liars? Truth is still   1450
The best and wisest. Lo! I went with him,
Thy husband, in attendance, to the height
Of yonder plain, where still all ruthlessly
The corpse of Polynices tombless lay,

Mangled by dogs. And, having prayed to her,
The Goddess of all pathways,[28] and to Pluto,
To look with favour on them, him they washed
With holy water; and what yet was left
We burnt in branches freshly cut, and heaped
A high raised grave from out the soil around,   1460
And then we entered on the stone-paved home,
Death's marriage-chamber for the ill-starred maid.
And some one hears, while standing yet afar,
Shrill voice of wailing near the bridal bower,
By funeral rites unhallowed, and he comes
And tells my master, Creon. On his ears,
Advancing nearer, falls a shriek confused
Of bitter sorrow, and with grieving loud,
He utters one sad cry: "Me miserable!
And am I, then, a prophet? Do I wend   1470
This day the dreariest way of all my life?
My son's voice greets me. Go, my servants, go,
Quickly draw near, and standing by the tomb,
Search ye and see; and where the joined stones
Still leave an opening, look ye in, and say
If I hear Haemon's voice, or if my soul
Is cheated by the Gods." And then we searched,
As he, our master, in his frenzy, bade us;
And, in the furthest corner of the vault,
We saw her hanging by a twisted cord   1480
Of linen threads entwined, and him we found
Clasping her form in passionate embrace,
And mourning o'er the doom that robbed him of her,
His father's deed, and that his marriage bed,
So full of sorrow. When he saw him there,
Groaning again in bitterness of heart,
He goes to him, and calls in wailing voice,
"Ah! wretched me! what dost thou! Hast thou lost
Thy reason? In what evil sinkest thou?
Come forth, my child, on bended knee I ask thee."   1490
And then the boy, with fierce, wild gleaming eyes,
Glared at him, spat upon his face, and draws,
Still answering naught, the sharp two-edged sword.
Missing his aim (his father from the blow
Turning aside), in anger with himself,

---

[28] Hecate, more or less identified with Persephone, and named here as the Goddess
who, being the guardian of highways, was wroth with Thebes for the pollution caused by
the unburied corpse of Polyneikes.

The poor ill-doomed one, even as he was,
Fell on his sword, and drove it through his breast,
Full half its length, and clasping, yet alive,
The maiden's arm, still soft, he there breathes out
In broken gasps, upon her fair white cheek,   1500
A rain of blood. And so at last they lie,
Dead bridegroom with dead bride, and he has gained
His marriage rites in Hades' darksome home,
And left to all men witness terrible,
That man's worst ill is stubbornness of heart.

[*Exit* EURYDICE.]

CHORUS. What dost thou make of this? She turns again,
     And not one word, or good or ill, will speak.
MESSENGER. I, too, am full of wonder. Yet with hopes
     I feed myself, she will not think it meet,
     Hearing her son's woes, openly to wail   1510
     Before her subjects, but beneath her roof
     Will think it best to bear her private griefs.
     Too trained a judgment has she so to err.
CHORUS. I know not. To my mind, or silence hard,
     Or vain wild cries, are signs of bitter woe.
MESSENGER. Soon we shall know, within the house advancing,
     If, in the passion of her heart, she hides
     A secret purpose. Truly dost thou speak;
     There is a terror in that silence hard.
CHORUS. [*seeing* CREON *approaching with the corpse of* Haemon *in
     his arms*]
     And, lo! the king himself comes on,   1520
     And in his hands he bears a record clear,
     No woe (if I may speak) by others caused,
     Himself the great offender.

[*Enter* CREON *bearing* Haemon'S *body.*]

CREON. Woe! for the sins of souls of evil mood,
     Strong, mighty to destroy;
     O ye who look on those of kindred race,
     The slayers and the slain,
Woe for mine own rash plans that prosper not;
Woe for thee, son; but new in life's career,
     And by a new fate dying.   1530
       Woe! woe!
     Thou diest, thou art gone,

Not by thine evil counsel, but by mine.
CHORUS. Ah me! Too late thou seem'st to see the right.
CREON. Ah me!
    I learn the grievous lesson. On my head,
    God, pressing sore, hath smitten me and vexed,
    In ways most rough and terrible (ah me!),
    Shattering the joy, and trampling underfoot.
    Woe! woe! We toil for that which profits not.   1540

    [*Enter* SECOND MESSENGER]

SECOND MESSENGER. My master! thou, as one who hast full store,
    One source of sorrow bearest in thine arms,
    And others in thy house, too soon, it seems,
    Thou need'st must come and see.
CREON. And what remains
    Worse evil than the evils that we bear?
SECOND MESSENGER. Thy wife is dead. Thy dead son's mother
      true,
    Ill starred one, smitten with a deadly blow,
    But some few moments since.
CREON. O agony?   1550
    Thou house of Death, that none may purify,
    Why dost thou thus destroy me?
    O thou who comest, bringing in thy train
    Woes horrible to tell,
    Thou tramplest on a man already slain.
    What say'st thou? What new tidings bring'st to me?
    Ah me! ah me!
    Is it that over all the slaughter wrought
    My own wife's death has come to crown it all?
CHORUS. It is but all too clear! No longer now   1560
    Does yon recess conceal her.

    [*The gates open and show the dead body of* EURYDICE.]

CREON. Woe is me!
    This second stroke I gaze on, miserable,
    What fate, yea, what still lies in wait for me?
    Here in my arms I bear what was my son;
    And there, O misery! look upon the dead.
    Ah, wretched mother! ah, my son! my son!
SECOND MESSENGER. Sore wounded, she around the altar clung,
    And closed her darkening eyelids, and bewailed

The honoured bed of Megareus,[29] who died   1570
Long since, and then again that corpse thou hast;
And last of all she cried a bitter cry
Against thy deeds, the murderer of thy son.
CREON. Woe! woe! alas!
    I shudder in my fear: Will no one strike
    A deadly blow with sharp two-edgèd sword?
    Fearful my fate, alas!
    And with a fearful woe full sore beset.
SECOND MESSENGER. She in her death charged thee with being the
        cause
    Of all their sorrows, his and hers alike.   1580
CREON. And in what way struck she the murderous blow?
SECOND MESSENGER. With her own hand below her
        heart she stabbed,
    Hearing her son's most pitiable fate.
CREON. Ah me! The fault is mine. On no one else,
    Of all that live, the fearful guilt can come;
    I, even I, did slay thee, wretched one,
    I; yes, I say it clearly. Come, ye guards,
    Lead me forth quickly; lead me out of sight,
    More crushed to nothing than the dead unborn.   1590
CHORUS. Thou counsellest gain, if gain there be in ills,
    For present evils then are easiest borne
    When shortest lived.
CREON. Oh, come thou, then, come thou,
    Last of my sorrows, that shall bring to me
    Best boon, my life's last day. Come, then, oh, come
    That nevermore I look upon the light.
CHORUS. These things are in the future. What is near,
    That we must do. O'er what is yet to come
    They watch, to whom that work of right belongs.   1600
CREON. I did but pray for what I most desire.
CHORUS. Pray thou for nothing more. For mortal man
    There is no issue from a doom decreed.
CREON. [*Looking at the two corpses*] Lead me, then, forth, vain
        shadow that I am,
    Who slew thee, O my son, unwittingly,
    And thee, too—(O my sorrow)—and I know not
    Which way to look. All near at hand is turned
    Aside to evil; and upon my head
    There falls a doom far worse than I can bear.

---

[29] In the legend which Sophocles follows, Megareus, a son of Creon and Eurydike, had been offered up as a sacrifice to save the state from its dangers.

CHORUS. Man's highest blessedness   1610
    In wisdom chiefly stands;
   And in the things that touch upon the Gods,
   'Tis best in word of deed
     To shun unholy pride;
   Great words of boasting bring great punishments;
   And so to gray-haired age
   Comes wisdom at the last.

THE END

Made in United States
Orlando, FL
28 July 2023

35547463R00043